Gourd Fun for everyone

Sammie Crawford, the Fairy Gourdmother™

4880 Lower Valley Road, Atglen, Pennsylvania 19310

ABOUT THE AUTHOR

Sammie Crawford, The Fairy Gourdmother™, was born and raised in Benton, Arkansas. She married her high school sweetheart, Harry, in 1966. She has worked in an office and as a landscape designer, but her favorite job was working as an artist with an advertising firm in Little Rock, Arkansas.

Always artistic, Sammie began decorative painting in 1987. In 1990, the Crawfords retired and moved to Hot Springs, Arkansas, where Sammie teaches decorative painting classes.

Several of Sammie's decorative painting designs have been published by national craft magazines, and Sammie became a Delta Associate Designer in 1997.

Sammie has appeared three times on *Willard Scott's Almanac* on Home & Garden Television (HGTV). Her gourd ornaments were hung on the White House Christmas tree in 1993, 1998 and 1999. These are now in the permanent collection of the Smithsonian Institution.

One day in 1993, a member of Sammie's painting club, Designing Women, suggested painting a gourd. That was the beginning of the love affair between Sammie and her gourds. But it wasn't love at first sight! Her first reaction was, "Who the heck wants to paint a gourd?" Now the gourds tell her who they are and give inspiration by their shape and size. Sammie's painting name, The Fairy Gourdmother, is a registered trademark.

Copyright © 2008 by Sammie Crawford
Library of Congress Control Number: 2008933700

ISBN: 978-0-7643-3124-4

Printed in China

Schiffer Books are available at special discounts for bulk purchases for sales promotions or premiums. Special editions, including personalized covers, corporate imprints, and excerpts can be created in large quantities for special needs. For more information contact the publisher.

Published by Schiffer Publishing Ltd.
4880 Lower Valley Road
Atglen, PA 19310
Phone: (610) 593-1777; Fax: (610) 593-2002
E-mail: Info@schifferbooks.com

For the largest selection of fine reference books on this and related subjects, please visit our web site at:
www.schifferbooks.com
We are always looking for people to write books on new and related subjects. If you have an idea for a book please contact us at the above address.

This book may be purchased from the publisher.
Include $5.00 for shipping.
Please try your bookstore first.
You may write for a free catalog.

In Europe, Schiffer books are distributed by
Bushwood Books
6 Marksbury Ave.
Kew Gardens
Surrey TW9 4JF England
Phone: 44 (0) 20 8392-8585; Fax: 44 (0) 20 8392-9876
E-mail: info@bushwoodbooks.co.uk
Website: www.bushwoodbooks.co.uk
Free postage in the U.K., Europe; air mail at cost.

DEDICATION

This book is dedicated to the memory of my mother, Freda Howe Rucker. She always knew I could.

ACKNOWLEDGMENTS

Thanks to the many friends who encouraged me all along the way.

My first teacher, Dolly Garner, who gave me a good, solid start.

The person who put the first gourd in my hands, Mary Ciontea. Little did we know, eh, Mary?

All my students who let me hone my skills on them. I hope they enjoyed it as much as I did.

My husband, Harry, my biggest fan and critic. He keeps me centered.

My editor, Greg Albert. Thanks for seeing the possibilities, Greg.

And all the other fine folks at North Light who helped me make this book a reality.

Editors: Jane Friedman and Nicole R. Klungle
Designer: Brian Roeth
Cover designer: Wendy Dunning
Production artist: Tari Sasser
Production coordinator: Sara Dumford
Photography: Christine Polomsky and Al Parrish

I highly recommend membership in both the American Gourd Society, 317 Maple Court, Kokomo, Indiana 46902-3633, and the National Society of Decorative Painters, 393 McLean Blvd., Wichita, Kansas 67203-5968. Both of these fine organizations deserve your support and you will benefit greatly from the association.

table of contents

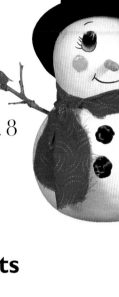

part *one*
Step-by-Step Projects

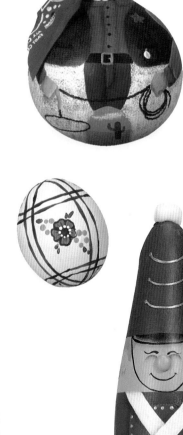

part *two*
Gallery

introduction

Gourds have been cultivated for hundreds of years. They have been used as music-makers, medicines, utensils, masks and clothing—and for many other purposes.

Over the past several years, gourds have grown steadily in popularity as a painting surface, and gourd craft continues to expand in the crafting world. When I began painting gourds in the early 1990s, hardly anyone was doing it. Now you can't enter a craft store or go to a craft fair without seeing painted, carved, woodburned or otherwise decorated gourds. The Internet is full of gourd Web sites, and there are some really clever "gourders" out there. There are also farms from California to Virginia that grow nothing but gourds. This is a booming enterprise, so now that we know we have a plentiful supply, grab some gourds, folks, and let's get busy!

Painting Terms & Techniques

The terms and techniques defined and illustrated in this section will help you complete your gourd projects successfully.

Back-to-back float. See *double float*.

Basecoat. This is the first coat of paint, the basis or background of your piece. You want to get good, smooth coverage without ridges because any mistakes here will show no matter what you do later. It is always best to apply several thin coats of paint rather than a heavy one. Remember to always allow the last coat to dry completely before proceeding. Otherwise the paint will lift and you are back to square one.

Brush blending. Loading one color onto your brush and stroking it on the palette to evenly distribute color, or loading two or more colors side by side on the brush and stroking to blend.

Bullseye. Floating color in a circle with the hard edge in the center, producing a halo.

C-stroke. A C-shaped brushstroke facing either left or right.

Chisel edge. The knife edge of your flat brush, used to produce a thin stroke.

Comma stroke. A comma-shaped brushstroke made by pressing slightly on the bristles when starting the stroke, then lifting the brush while stroking downward. Can be made to face right or left.

Crackle medium. Products brushed on between contrasting coats of color that cause the top coat to crackle, letting the bottom color show through: This results in a weathered or old look.

Dabbing. Using an old "scruffy brush" or deerfoot to fill in leaves, bushes, etc. Same as *pouncing*.

Dip dot. A dot of paint produced by using the end of the stylus or brush handle to make round objects such as flower centers and high-lights in eyes.

Dirty brush. Going from one color to the next without cleaning your brush. This method is sometimes used to carry some of the same colors throughout the painting.

Dolly Parton heart. This is a small heart produced by placing two dip dots side by side and joining them by drawing a V between them. Also known as a *dip dot* heart.

Double float. This is a technique where you pull a *float* and then turn your brush over (or your piece) and place a second float next to it so that the two hard edges touch. It is most often used to highlight items such as the shine on a ribbon. It is the same as *flip float*, *reverse float*, *mirror float* or *back-to-back float*.

Double load. Dip one corner of your brush in one color and the other corner in a second color. Work the brush, blending the two colors together.

Dress. Moisten your brush, apply paint and stroke the brush on the palette to evenly distribute the color. (Don't leave too much water in the brush—just dampen it.)

Drybrush. Dress the brush with paint

Floating, or Side-Loading a Brush

1 To float or side-load, moisten your brush in clean water and blot it just until it loses its shine. Leave as much water as possible without it being drippy.

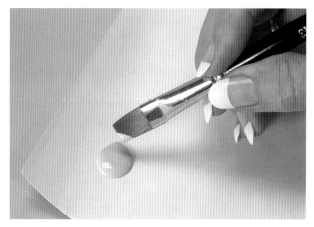

2 Touch the corner of the brush in the paint.

3 Apply slight pressure and work the brush back and forth on the palette, blending the color and allowing it to travel across the brush.

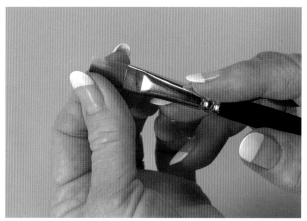

4 Flip the brush over and gently pinch off the excess water. The clean side of the brush can be used as an "eraser" to pick up small errors.

and then blend it on your palette or towel until only a little paint remains. If you leave too much, the area will only look basecoated. It is better to start light and build up as needed. Keep it light.

Extender. Used to extend drying time. May be used in place of water when floating. Also called *retarder*. These mediums may be brushed across the surface or mixed in the paint.

Ferrule. This is the metal part of the brush that holds the bristles in place.

Flip float. See *double float*.

Float. This stroke is the backbone of decorative painting. Dip your brush in clean water and blot it on a paper towel only until the brush loses its shine. Turn your brush up on edge and dip one corner in the paint. Work it flat back and forth on the palette, pressing down and blending the color across the brush until it fades to nothing. Keep the clean side of your brush paint free. Gently remove any excess water from the clean side by pinching it off with your fingers. Gently! Now you're ready to float a shadow or highlight. Keep the brush flat on the surface or you will not get the desired effect, just a hard line. Don't try to cheat by going back for more paint when you run out without first rinsing your brush and reloading it from scratch: That will only produce a harsh line, not a float. This stroke is also called *shading* or *side loading*.

Flow medium. This is added to your water, brush or paint to give smooth, even coverage on your painting surface. Especially helpful when painting long, thin strokes with your liner brush.

Fly specking. See *spattering*.

Gesso. (pronounced "jesso") Usually a white opaque medium used to prime surfaces, gesso seals and provides *tooth*. It is useful in blocking undesirable colors.

Glaze. If you wish to lighten or darken a section of your painting, water down the paint to the consistency of ink. Use glaze where you wish to change the underlying color slightly.

Glazing medium. This medium may be used in place of water when glazing. It simply increases the transparency of the paint.

Gold leaf. Extremely thin sheets of genuine gold applied over an adhesive to give a gilded look. Leaf is also available in powder and liquid forms and in other colors, such as silver and copper. It can be antiqued to produce an older look.

Gouache. (pronounced "gwash") A paint containing chalk to make it more opaque. May be used the same way as acrylics or as a watercolor when thinned.

Hard edge. Refers to the corner of the brush the paint is on when preparing to *float*. The soft edge is the clean side.

Liner brush. A thin brush with a rounded tip used for creating fine lines and narrow strokes.

Loading. See *dress*.

Masking. Covering a portion of the piece to protect it from unwanted paint. This may be done with a piece of paper or tape, or by using masking fluids if warranted.

Mirror float. See *double float*.

Mop, mopping. A fluffy brush used to lightly soften a hard paint edge.

Pickling/pickling stain. This medium is used to give your piece a whitish look while allowing the grain of the wood to show through. It can also be used with a hint of color.

Primer. A coating used to seal porous surfaces, to cover unwanted colors or, when used on metal, to provide *tooth* and inhibit rust.

Pouncing. See *stippling*.

Pull. Using your liner brush to add or "pull" individual wispy lines. This term is usually used in regard to hair or fur.

Rake brush. A brush with several extra-long bristles used to create the fine lines of hair or fur.

Retarder. See *extender*.

Reverse float. See *double float*.

Scruffy brush. You can't buy this brush: You have to *earn* it. It is simply a worn-out brush used for dabbing in greenery, fur, etc. Don't worry—you'll have plenty of them if you don't take good care of your brushes!

Sealer. A waterproof medium used to seal the surface prior to painting to block resins, prevent the grain of wood from rising and provide a general overall smooth painting surface. Light sanding may be required once the sealer has dried. Do not confuse this with finishing sealers more commonly called *varnish*.

Shading. See *float*.

Side load. Same as *floating*. Remember that you want a nice fade across your brush from color on one side to just clear water on the other side.

Sitdown. This is a stroke used to produce small leaves, etc. It works just as the name implies: Dress a small round brush with paint and touch or "sit down" on the surface. This produces a small oval leaf when slight pressure is applied.

Slip-slap. Criss-cross, overlapping strokes applied in a loose, random manner.

Soft edge. Refers to the clean side of

Using a Liner Brush

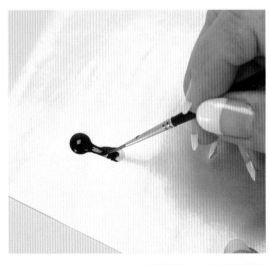

1 When using a liner brush, always thin the paint to the consistency of ink. Do this by pulling a small amount of paint into a puddle of water from your brush.

2 When the brush is dressed, pull it across the palette, rotating it between your fingers to bring it back to a point. Regular liners are fine for making comma strokes, etc., but for long lines, try a script liner.

Using Your Rake Brush

1 Moisten your brush with water and blot on a paper towel. Dress the brush with paint by dipping the bristles in the paint and stroking the brush back and forth on the palette to distribute the paint evenly. Then set the brush down on the palette and fan the bristles out by applying slight pressure and rotating the brush between your fingers.

2 If you have the right amount of water in the brush, a light brush stroke will now produce several fine lines. Too much water makes a solid stroke, too little water and the paint refuses to flow off the brush. This takes practice, but it is well worth the effort. There is no substitute for the rake for making hair and fur.

the brush when it is dressed to float, as opposed to the hard edge, which carries the paint.

Spattering. Load your fan brush or an old toothbrush with thinned paint. Test it first to be sure it isn't too watery, then hold the brush several inches above the surface and pull your finger across the bristles to achieve a speckled look. I usually pull mine across the handle of another brush—keeps my nails

cleaner. This is also known as *fly specking*.

Sponge. Using a sponge to produce a textured appearance. Different kinds of sponges yield different effects. Silk sponges are finer and have smaller holes than sea sponges. Com-pressed sponges are manmade and create yet another effect. Sponges can also be cut into varying shapes. First saturate and soften the sponge in clean water. Squeeze (never wring) all excess water out and then roll the sponge in a paper towel. Dab a small amount of paint on and then pounce on the palette, removing excess paint. As you sponge and the paint begins to run out, don't press harder. This simply produces a smudged effect. Reapply the paint, again pouncing the excess off on the palette, and continue.

Always rinse the sponge immediately after use, or you wind up with a hard, useless sponge—and they're not cheap. If you can't

stop to rinse, toss used sponges into your water tub.

Stippling. Using a scruffy or deerfoot brush to produce texture. Most often used to make fur, foliage or a dappled effect. You use this brush somewhat like your sponge. Dip a dry deerfoot into a small amount of paint and pounce the excess off on the palette or a paper towel. Too much paint results in solid coverage and defeats the purpose. Pounce the brush straight up and down on the piece and allow it to dry. Repeat if necessary, don't try to achieve density all in one move.

Stylus. A handle with a small metal ball tip on each end, used to transfer patterns or to make small, round dots. When using a stylus to make dots, always save the dots for last as it takes them a long time to dry.

Tack cloth. A piece of cheesecloth treated to make it sticky. It is used to pick up dust after sanding along with any unwanted dirt or dust before painting. Do not use it between coats, because it could leave unwanted deposits.

Tinting. See *glazing*.

Tooth. Refers to the texture or lack of texture a surface has, which determines how paint will adhere. Glass and metal have very little tooth, making priming necessary to provide the needed texture.

Transfer. Transferring the pattern to the painting surface using a stylus. Do not bear down. This will score your surface, leaving unwanted impressions.

Transfer paper. Specially coated paper used between the pattern and the surface. Carbon paper cannot be substituted. It is oil based and would leave a film that could repel paint. New transfer paper tends to leave a mess, especially the black. I've found that turning the new paper over and gently rubbing it with a

paper towel removes a great deal of the excess carbon. The older the paper, the better. I have some I've been using for several years. As long as it produces images, it's good. If you don't have access to transfer paper, you can make your own by turning your pattern over and retracing the lines with a charcoal pencil, chalk or even a graphite pencil.

Triple load. This is when you dress your brush in a base color, then dip each corner in complementary shades, one light and one dark. Work the brush as in blending to float. You should have a nice progression fading from light to dark across the brush.

Undercoat. The coat applied before a transparent layer is added.

Varnish. A final protective coating that seals a surface against dirt and damage. There are spray and brush-

on varnishes available in matte, satin or gloss finishes. I like about three coats, each applied lightly, with plenty of drying time allowed between coats. Sand between coats with a piece of brown grocery sack or 600 sandpaper. Wipe gently with a tack cloth. Don't sand the last coat.

Walking color. Moisten your surface with water or extender. With the hard edge on the left, float a stroke, lift the brush and move it very slightly to the right, and repeat. Continue moving and stroking to the right, applying less pressure each time.

Wet on wet. Working wet paint onto the first coat while it is still wet to blend the colors. This must be done before the first coat begins to dry. *Extender* is useful here.

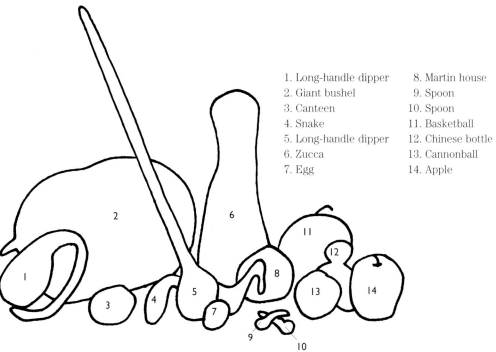

1. Long-handle dipper
2. Giant bushel
3. Canteen
4. Snake
5. Long-handle dipper
6. Zucca
7. Egg
8. Martin house
9. Spoon
10. Spoon
11. Basketball
12. Chinese bottle
13. Cannonball
14. Apple

Getting Started

This section will tell you what you will need to get started in painting gourds and how to prepare a gourd to paint. I'm not going to get into the growing end of it—that's a whole different book—but I will tell you how to dry, clean and prep your gourds.

These are the basic supplies you will need to complete the projects in this book. The specific supplies used for each project will be listed before the instructions for that project.

All of the gourds used in this book are from

Dalton Farms
610 CR 336
Piggott, AR 72454
ddalton@piggott.net
www.pumpkinhollow.com
(870) 598-3568

tools and materials

Gourd Prep Materials
- Dap Fast 'n Final Spackle
- fine sandpaper
- tack cloth
- Delta Ceramcoat Waterbased Sealer

For Transferring Patterns
- pencil
- stylus
- tracing paper
- black transfer paper
- white transfer paper

Painting Supplies
- Job Squad brand paper towels
- Loew-Cornell water tub
- palette paper
- sea and silk sponges
- Q-Tip brand cotton swabs
- Delta Ceramcoat Color Float
- Delta Brush Cleaner
- glue gun
- blow dryer
- Delta Ceramcoat acrylics

Finishing Sprays
- Delta Acrylic Gloss Finish Spray
- Delta Ceramcoat Satin Interior Spray Varnish
- Delta Ceramcoat Matte Interior Spray Varnish

Miscellaneous Supplies
- white pastel pencil
- gray pastel pencil
- FIMO polymer clay
- Delta Quick 'n Tacky glue

Loew-Cornell Brushes
- Series 7050 nos. 1 and 10/0 script liners
- Series 7120 ½" rake brush
- Series 7300 nos. 2, 4, 6, 8 and 12 flat shaders
- Series 7500 nos. 2, 4, 6 and 8 filberts
- Series 7520 ½" filbert rake
- Series 7550 1" wash brush
- Series 7850 ⅛" and ¼" deerfoot
- no. 32 fan brush
- no. 275 mop brush

Tools and Materials

CARING FOR YOUR BRUSHES

To do a first-rate job, you must use first-rate tools. Even though your brushes will be your most expensive investment, you cannot do a good job with cheap brushes. If you take good care of your brushes, they will last a long time and be worth what you put into them.

Never let the paint get up into the ferrule. If you are basecoating a large piece and you see the paint is starting to creep up the bristles, stop and clean the brush. There is no rule that says you must do all the painting in one sitting. The same thing applies if the paint starts to dry on the bristles after you have been painting for some time. Just stop, clean the brush and go again.

If the paint *does* get into the ferrule, use a good brush cleaner and work it well into the bristles. Rinse and repeat as many times as it takes to make the water run clear. I like to blot the brush on a clean paper towel, applying a slight pressure. If there is any paint left, it will show on the towel.

Forgot and left paint to dry in the brush? Usually you can soak the brush in cleaner for several hours or overnight and it will break up the paint. *Don't* stand the brush on its bristles. Suspend it over the cleaner. If you don't have a "store bought" holder, put the handle through a piece of cardboard and lay the cardboard across the top of the container holding the cleaner. Or save the plastic cover from your "to go" soft drink and push the brush through the hole where the straw would go. Just be sure the bristles don't touch the bottom of the container.

If that doesn't work, the brush is lost anyway, so try soaking it in nail polish remover. This usually works when all else fails. If not, you have

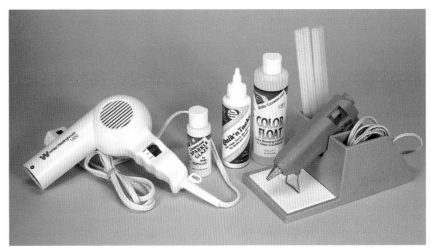

From left to right: blow dryer, Delta Ceramcoat Sparkle Glaze, Delta Quick 'n Tacky Glue, Delta Ceramcoat Color Float, glue gun with glue sticks.

A metal palette knife and various brushes

just earned yourself a scruffy brush. Use it to make foliage and fuzzy things.

PALETTE PAPER

One of the things on your list of supplies is palette paper. I buy the 9" × 12" bound tablets to carry with me when I travel, but I find that a roll of freezer paper works just fine at home. I just tear off a piece and tape it to my desktop—and it's a whole lot cheaper.

PAPER TOWELS

I called for Job Squad brand paper towels specifically. I know there are cheaper brands of paper towels on the market, but none of them can hold a candle to Job Squad for absorbency—and your towel will be required to hold a lot of water. You can use another brand, but you will use a lot more of them!

WATER TUBS

If you are not going to invest in a brush tub at first, you can use plastic tubs for water. Just be sure to use two, one for clean water and one for dirty water, and change the water often. You will see what I mean the first time you go from red to white paint and don't wash in the "dirty" tub and then rinse your brush in the "clean" tub. Always start with clean water in your brush.

BLOW DRYERS

I have found a blow dryer to be a good friend. When using it, be sure to keep it moving. It doesn't take long to get your piece hot enough to blister the paint. I keep my hand where it will be hit by the air from the dryer when blowing. If it gets too hot for my hand, you can bet it's too hot for the paint.

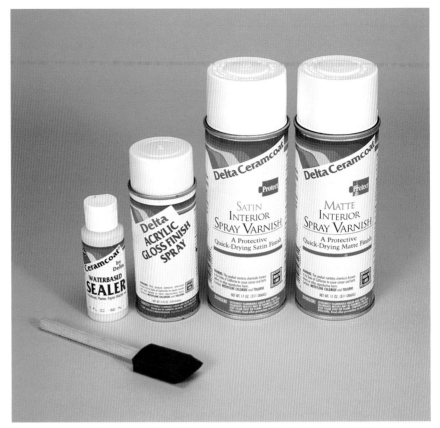

Sealers and varnishes, from left to right: sponge brush, Delta Ceramcoat Waterbased Sealer, Delta Acrylic Gloss Finish Spray, Delta Ceramcoat Satin Interior Spray Varnish, Delta Ceramcoat Matte Interior Spray Varnish.

VARNISHES

There are many fine varnishes on the market, but I guess you stay with what you start with. My first teacher started me with spray varnish and I've never strayed. Being the impatient type, I've found it suits my needs best. A lot of people swear by the brush-on type—you won't know which you prefer until you try them both.

Consider, too, the different types of finishes: satin, matte and gloss. Each has its place, and you will probably use them all. I prefer to use the satin and matte finishes on my animals and people, reserving the gloss for things such as metal, balloons and other shiny surfaces.

Preparing Your Gourds for Painting

DRYING YOUR GOURDS

If you grow your own gourds, the easiest way to dry them is to just leave them on the vine through the winter. Normally I buy my gourds already dried, but sometimes that special gourd comes along and I can't wait. I grab it while I can and dry it myself. I am fortunate to have a space between my carport railing and a chain link fence where I can string a length of chicken wire and make a "hammock" for my green gourds. It is essential that there is plenty of air circulation and sunshine around them. Don't forget how heavy they are when green. I overloaded that hammock once and almost pulled the fence down. If you don't have a place like mine, put them out in the yard where the sun can get to them and put them on wooden palettes. The air can still circulate under them and they will dry.

Green gourds are about 90 percent water. This water has to evaporate through the shell. In the process, the gourds will turn black and moldy. It is at this point that first-time gourders throw them away, thinking that they have been ruined. They are just now getting good. If the gourd shrivels up, develops holes or gets mushy, throw it away immediately to avoid contaminating the others. Otherwise, just be patient. It takes varying lengths of time for gourds to dry, depending on the size of the gourd. An egg gourd will dry in a week. A giant bushel can take months. But they all must turn black and yucky to dry.

To clean a dry gourd for painting, soak it in the kitchen sink in a few inches of water and about ¼ cup of household bleach. Scrubbing with a nylon mesh scrubber pad will get 98 percent of the mold off. As you can see in the photo, I had my husband modify a small paring knife until only a couple inches of the blade remained. This makes a handy tool for scraping off that last little bit of stubborn mold and skin.

I let the gourd dry 24 hours before sealing and painting unless I'm in a hurry. If I can't wait, I put it in the oven at 200°F for half an hour and it's ready to go. If you wish, apply wood sealer as insurance against any missed mold.

WASHING YOUR GOURDS

When your gourds are light and the seeds rattle inside, they are dry. The seeds don't always rattle, but you can still tell if it's ready by the weight. At this point, take them in the house and soak them in the sink in about ¼ cup of bleach and a couple of inches of water. After soaking for ten minutes or so, that mold will come off fairly easy using a plastic scrubber pad. If there are stubborn spots, I use a dull paring knife to scrape them off. It is imperative that you remove *all* of the mold and fungus because it can grow back and cause your paint to flake off.

Sanding and Sealing Your Gourds

To prepare your gourd for painting, you'll need Dap spackle, fine sandpaper, a tack cloth, Delta Ceramcoat Waterbased Sealer and a sponge brush.

Once your gourd is clean and dry, inspect it for any flaws. Some folks feel that a blemish or two adds character, but I like to sand off any bumps and fill the holes. I think it just looks better if Farmer John doesn't have a big hole where his nose should be!

I use spackle to fill the holes because it doesn't shrink or crack and it can be sanded and painted.

If the bumps are larger than I can handle with sandpaper, I use the belt sander in my shop to *lightly* remove them. Be careful not to apply too much pressure, or you will have a different problem to mend.

Applying a Pattern

You'll need tracing paper, transfer paper, a pencil and a stylus. Enlarge the pattern to fit your gourd. Your patterns may need to be adjusted to follow the size and contours of your particular gourd.

Once you pick a pattern, place the tracing paper over the design and copy it using the pencil. When finished, place the pattern in position on your gourd. Lift the corner of your pattern and slip the transfer paper underneath it. Use the stylus to make a couple of marks and then check to be sure you don't have the transfer paper upside down. (I wish I had a nickel for every time I've done *that*.) Continue using the stylus to trace over the rest of the pattern.

Another way to transfer is to apply charcoal or pastel to the back of your tracing and use the stylus to trace. I sometimes use this method on faces. This eliminates the need for graphite (transfer) paper, but there are situations where it isn't practical. Also, it

If you have a gourd that is less than a perfect "sitter," modify it by slicing the bottom off with a bandsaw. Draw around the portion you cut off and, allowing for the thickness of the shell, cut a piece of plywood to fit the hole. It will take a little fine tuning, but you *can* get a good fit. Once you have glued the plywood in place using wood glue and it's dry, fill any cracks with spackle. When this is dry, you can sand and paint it and the modification is completely undetectable.

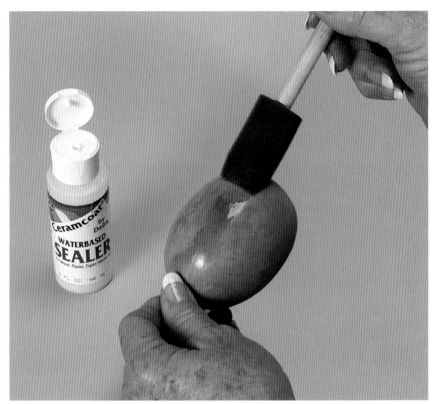

Once the spackle is dry, lightly sand and then remove dust with a tack cloth. Now you're ready to apply wood sealer. Apply the sealer with a sponge brush. Do not rinse the brush when finished; just let it dry and keep it for use with the sealer only. When you reapply sealer to it, it will soften and be ready for use again.

doesn't stay on as well.

Transferring patterns to a rounded surface is sometime tricky: The easiest way to do it is to cut your pattern apart and apply the individual pieces one at a time. I find this is best when painting a cottage—it's much easier to position the doors and windows. You can freehand the ground level or

the roof edge if you like.

I usually apply the face pattern first, then the front of the clothes. If I need to make a level mark all the way around the gourd—for a belt or grass line, for instance—I rest my hand on something at the height I want the mark, hold the pencil stationary and turn the gourd, marking it as it turns.

Hints for Success With Your Gourds

1 If the gourd doesn't want to stand up, sometimes just shaking the seeds inside is all it takes. If it still doesn't stand, perhaps a little sanding on the bottom is needed. If all else fails, try the plywood bottom technique discussed on page 18.

2 If you are right handed, paint the left eye and brow on a face first. It is much easier to get them to match. You southpaws do just the opposite. I'm not sure why this works, but it does.

3 Never stand a wet brush on end. You may think you have gotten that brush perfectly clean but if there is even the slightest trace of paint left, it will run into the ferrule, where it can do a lot of damage. Soon you will have more scruffy brushes than you can use.

4 There is always an exception to every rule. We are taught to always dampen our brush before dressing it, but the deerfoot and the mop are used dry.

5 If you paint the eyes in solid white before adding the irises and pupils, it allows you to more easily see whether they are the same size and are level.

6 Whenever you see number like 2:1 or 1:3 after colors, it means the mixture ratio. For instance, white and blue 2:1 means two parts white to one part blue.

7 Always thin paint to an ink consistency when using a liner brush or rake brush. Otherwise, the paint doesn't flow off the bristles.

8 When starting a float or a border, start in the back if you have a choice. That way if your border doesn't quite come out even, it's not as noticeable.

9 Don't hold your breath when trying to paint a long line. Take a deep breath and slowly exhale as you pull the brush. Still catch yourself holding your breath? Then hum. You can't do both.

10 Is one of the eyes getting bigger than the other? Don't keep adding, trying to make them come out even. He will soon look like Barney Google! Go back to your base color with a liner brush and reduce the other one. Sometimes all it takes is a little line under the eye.

11 Ridges on the edge of your stroke? You're overloading your brush. That is why several thin coats are better than one thick one. Don't panic, though. Just use your finger to push the paint ridge back over on the wet painted area then proceed.

part one

Step-by-Step Projects

The projects in this chapter are accompanied by step-by-step painting instructions. After completing these projects, you'll not only have an impressive gallery of gourd characters, you'll also be able to start applying what you've learned to designing your own gourds. If you aren't quite ready for that, take inspiration from the projects in Part 2, starting on page 82. I've included patterns and general instructions for these gourds, and you will be able to use the techniques illustrated here to paint them.

bow-legged cowboy

materials

Delta Ceramcoat acrylics
- 14 K Gold
- Black
- Blue Heaven
- Burnt Umber
- Cinnamon
- Desert Sun Orange
- Ivory
- Lavender Lace
- Medium Flesh
- Midnight Blue
- Nightfall Blue
- Old Parchment
- Santa's Flesh
- Seminole Green
- Spice Brown
- Spice Tan
- Tide Pool Blue
- Trail Tan
- White

Loew-Cornell brushes
- Series 7050 10/0 liner
- Series 7300 no. 12 flat shader
- Series 7500 no. 4 filbert
- Series 7550 ¾" wash brush

Indonesian bottle gourd
Conte pastel stick in Sanguine
sponge
glue gun
cowboy hat
bandanna
Delta Waterbased Sealer
Delta Ceramcoat Color Float
Delta Ceramcoat Matte Interior
 Spray Varnish

This cowboy has spent too much time in the saddle! You can see the desert background right between his legs. The shape of the bottle gourd lends itself to this design, since the "bottle neck" creates a separation between the cowboy's head and body. Adding details to your gourd characters— such as this cowboy's star— makes them seem that much more alive.

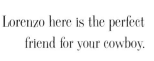

Lorenzo here is the perfect friend for your cowboy.

Enlarge this pattern to fit your gourd. Every pattern may require
adjustments to follow the contours of your particular gourd.

Gourd Fun for Everyone

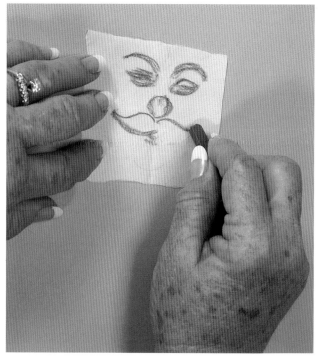

2 Create transfer pattern for details.

On the back of your pattern, retrace the lines using a pastel stick. The pastel stick will transfer to the gourd when you trace the pattern details from the front. I use the Conte brand crayon called Sanguine. It is water soluble and therefore won't remain once the details are painted.

1 Prepare and basecoat gourd.

Seal gourd and allow to dry. Apply the pattern, leaving out the details. Basecoat the head in Medium Flesh. Basecoat the vest in Spice Brown; the belt in Black; the shirt (minus the sleeves) in Tide Pool Blue; the pants in Nightfall Blue; the chaps in Old Parchment; the sky in Blue Heaven and the ground in Trail Tan.

This little boy is playing
"cowboys and Indians."

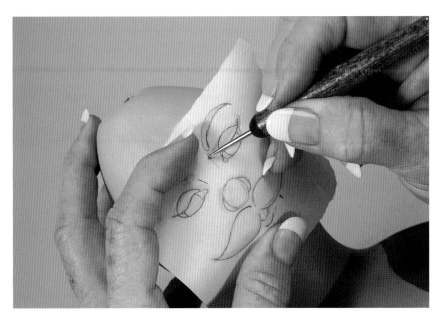

3 Trace the details.
Place the pattern on the gourd and trace it using your stylus.

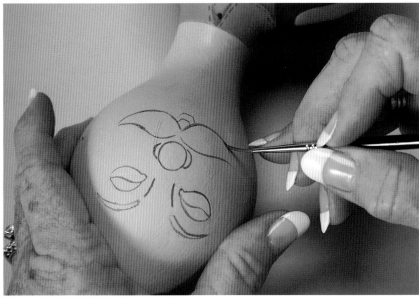

4 Outline the facial features.
Outline the features using the no. 10/0 liner and thinned Burnt Umber.

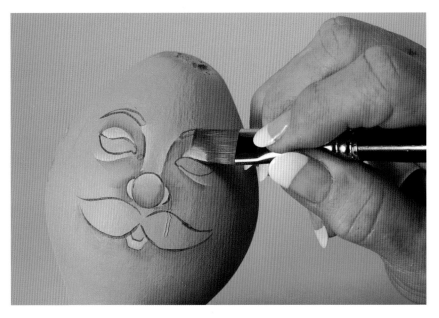

5 Highlight the facial features.
Using the no. 12 flat shader and Santa's Flesh, shade on each side of the nose on the nose, above the eyelid fading up, above the wrinkles under the eyes, on each nostril cover, across the top of the ball of the nose and on the lip.

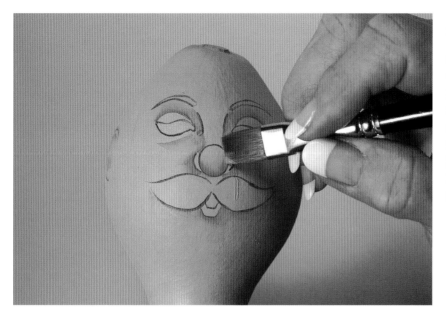

6 Shade the facial features.

Using the same no. 12 flat shader and Desert Sun Orange, shade down each side of the nose, above the eye fading up, under the mustache and mouth, under the wrinkles below the eyes and inside across the bottom of the ball of the nose. Paint the mouth in Cinnamon, the eyes in Tide Pool Blue (with Black pupils), and the eyebrows and mustache in Spice Brown.

7 Sponge the vest and chaps.

When the paint is dry, moisten a silk sponge and squeeze out (never wring out) the excess water. Roll the sponge in a paper towel and squeeze to remove even more water. Dab the sponge in a small amount of Burnt Umber and pounce any excess paint off on the palette. Pounce lightly on the vest to give a textured look; float Burnt Umber around the vest pockets as well. Pounce a thicker coat of Ivory on the cowboy's chaps.

8 Basecoat sleeves.

Basecoat the shirt sleeves with Tide Pool Blue. Always use the largest brush you can comfortably fit into a space. The larger the brush, the fewer the streaks.

9 Basecoat, shade and highlight hands.

Basecoat the hands with Medium Flesh. Shade across the tops of the hands with Santa's Flesh. Highlight along the bottoms of the hands and next to the shirt cuffs with Desert Sun Orange.

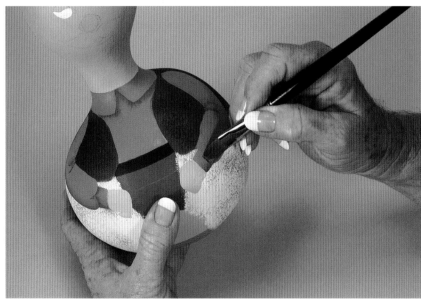

10 Shade the shirt.

Using the no. 12 flat shader and Nightfall Blue, shade the shirt under the collar, around the cuffs, along each side of the button placket, in the wrinkles and along the bottom of the sleeves.

11 Paint jeans pocket.

Add a back pocket to the jeans by outlining and shading with Midnight Blue.

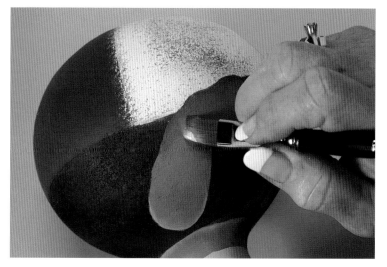

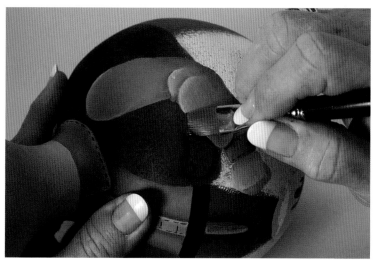

13 Paint cactus.
Using a filbert brush, fill in the cactus with Seminole Green.

12 Highlight shirt.
Using the no. 12 flat shader and Lavender Lace, highlight the shirt along the edges of the collar, down each side on top of the button placket, and along the top of the sleeves. Finish the wrinkles at the elbows by highlighting along the shading you did previously.

This Davy Crockett impersonator has a fake fur hat.*

*No raccoons were harmed in the painting of this gourd.

14 Add cloud.
Stipple in a cloud using White.

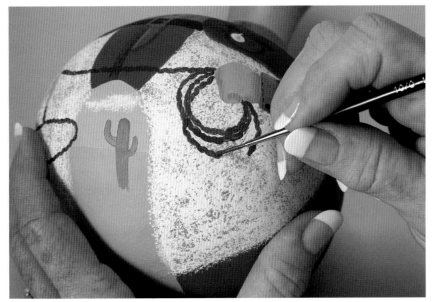

15 Paint the rope.
Paint the cowboy's rope with Spice Brown, and add details with Burnt Umber.

16 Add stitching details.
Using a 10/0 liner brush and thinned Midnight Blue, apply stitches to the collar, cuffs and shirt front.

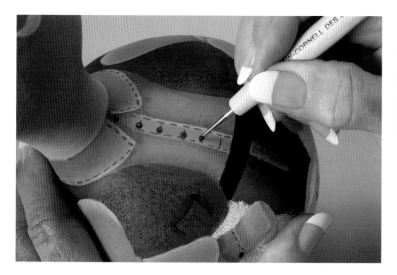

17 Paint buttons, star and belt buckle.

Using the large end of the stylus, make the buttons with Midnight Blue. Do this last because it takes any large dot of paint a long time to dry. Basecoat the star on the vest and the belt buckle in Trail Tan, then paint in 14K Gold. Add a pocket watch to the vest pocket if you like.

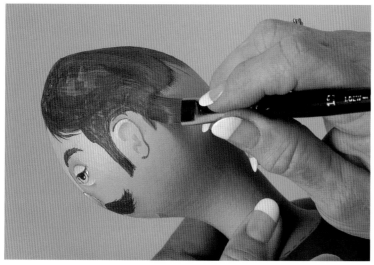

18 Basecoat the hair.

Basecoat the hair in using Spice Brown and a no. 12 flat. Pull little wispy hairs down from the forehead. Allow to dry.

19 Add hat and bandanna.

Spray with several light coats of varnish. Glue the hat in place. Cut a small triangle from a bandanna and tie it around the cowboy's neck.

The finished cowboy.

egg ornament

materials

Delta Ceramcoat acrylics
- Alpine Green
- Antique Rose
- Blue Heaven
- Custard
- Grape
- White

Loew-Cornell brushes
- Series 7050 10/0 script liner
- Series 7300 no. 12 flat shader
- Series 7500 no. 4 filbert

egg gourd
craft lathe
Delta Waterbased Sealer
Delta Ceramcoat Color Float
Delta Acrylic Gloss Finish Spray
stylus
ribbon for hanging ·
glue gun for attaching ribbon

This ornament, made from an egg gourd, can be used at Easter or on almost any occasion. You can also add it to the Easter Rabbit project on page 92. The stripes are simple to make using a craft lathe, a tool that holds the gourd on the ends and allows you to turn it while painting to keep the stripes even. If you don't have a craft lathe, paint the stripes by hand—because they are wavy, no one will notice if they're a little uneven. You can adapt the flower pattern on this egg to almost any purpose by varying the colors.

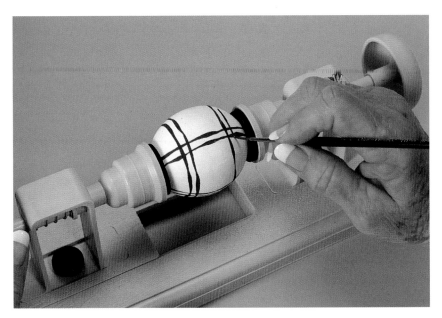

1 Basecoat gourd and paint stripes.

Seal gourd with wood sealer. Basecoat in white. When dry, place the egg end to end in lathe and use the liner brush and Grape to place stripes around egg. Vary your pressure to get the wiggly lines. When dry, place the egg crossways in the lathe and divide the egg into quarters, using the same color and method. You can also paint these stripes by hand.

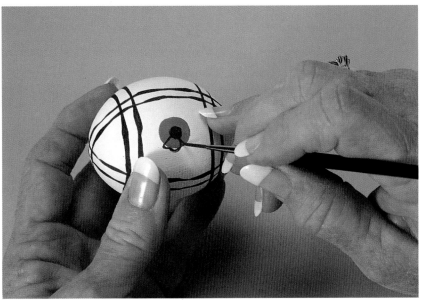

2 Paint large central flower.

Use the filbert to paint a small circle of Grape for the flower center. Paint a bullseye of Antique Rose around this circle. Use the liner brush and Grape to paint in the petals. They don't have to be perfect. Pull a couple of lines from the center as petal details.

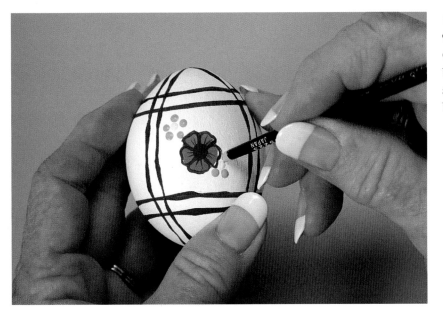

3 Paint small blue flowers.

Use the brush handle and Custard to make the centers of the blue flowers. Apply the petals the same way using Blue Heaven. Add blue flowers at both ends of the egg.

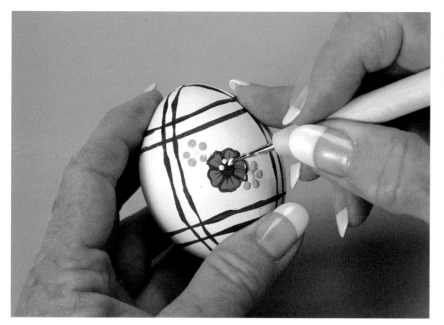

4 Detail central flower.

Use the stylus to place White dots around the center of the large flower. Avoid smearing these dots: They take a long time to dry, so always do them last.

5 Paint leaves.

Use the liner and Alpine Green to make the leaves. Simply touch the brush to the surface. These pinpoint strokes are called "sit downs." Apply several light coats of gloss spray finish.

The finished egg ornament.

farmer john

materials

Delta Ceramcoat acrylics
- Black
- Black Cherry
- Bridgeport Grey
- Burnt Sienna
- Candy Bar Brown
- Desert Sun Orange
- Fiesta Pink
- Medium Flesh
- Midnight Blue
- Nightfall Blue
- Rouge
- Santa's Flesh
- Straw
- Tide Pool Blue
- Tomato Spice
- White

Loew-Cornell brushes
- Series 7050 10/0 script liner
- Series 7300 nos. 2, 12 flat shaders
- Series 7520 ½"filbert rake
- Series 7550 ¾" wash

bottle gourd
small stalk of wheat
straw hat
doll glasses
glue gun
Delta Ceramcoat Color Float
Delta Waterbased Sealer
Delta Ceramcoat Satin Interior
  Spray Varnish

You can tell old Farmer John is a hayseed by the stalk of wheat between his teeth. Look for miniature hats and other accessories in the doll-making section of your local craft store.

This Wall Street banker must be Farmer John's "city cousin."

Enlarge this pattern to fit your gourd. Every pattern may require
adjustments to follow the contours of your particular gourd.

Gourd Fun for Everyone

1 Prepare and basecoat gourd.

Seal gourd and let dry. Apply pattern minus details. Basecoat hands and face Medium Flesh. Basecoat hair, brows and mustache Bridgeport Grey. Basecoat union suit Tomato Spice; coveralls are Nightfall Blue. Trace features; outline in Burnt Sienna.

2 Fill in the eyes.

Fill the eyes in with solid White. This allows you to better judge whether they are the same size and are level.

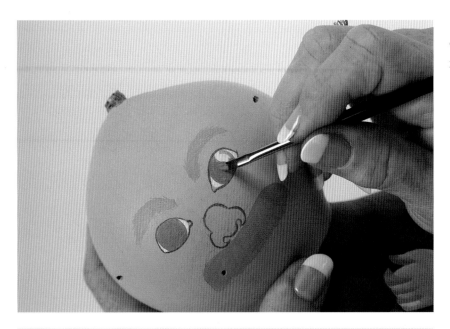

3 Paint irises.
Using a small filbert, fill in the irises with Tide Pool Blue.

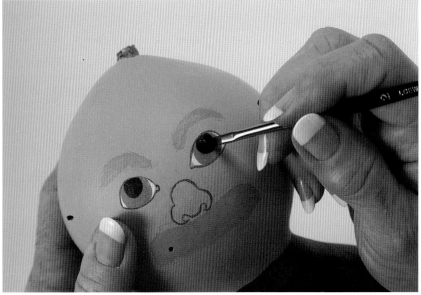

4 Add pupils.
Fill in the pupils with Black.

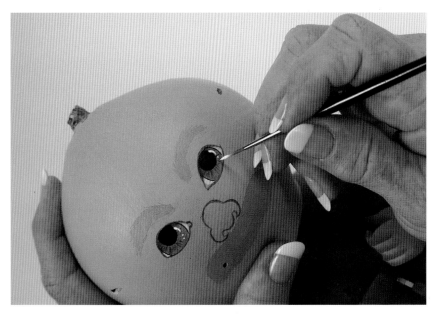

5 Make the eyes twinkle.
Use the liner brush and White to place a comma stroke in each eye for a highlight.

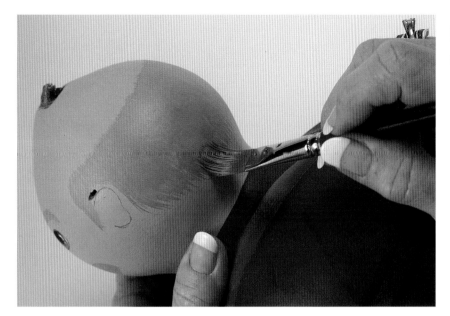

6 Basecoat the hair.
Basecoat the hair in Bridgeport Grey, keeping the edges shaggy.

7 Highlight hair in White.
Using the rake brush and White, suggest individual hairs. Repeat on the mustache.

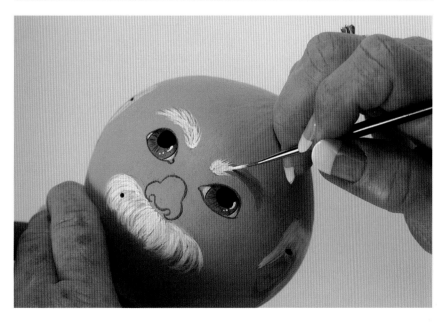

8 Highlight eyebrows.
Using the liner brush and White, fill in the eyebrows with short, choppy strokes. Be sure to pay attention to which way the hair grows.

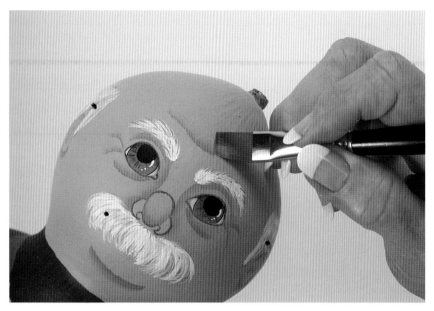

9 Shade face.

Use the no. 12 flat shader and Desert Sun Orange to shade all the wrinkles on the face. Float color down each side of the nose, across the forehead, across the bottom of the ball of the nose, at the wrinkles under the eyes and at the corners of the eyes. Float thinned Black across the eye under the eyelid for a shadow, being very careful. This is a strong color and you want just a shadow.

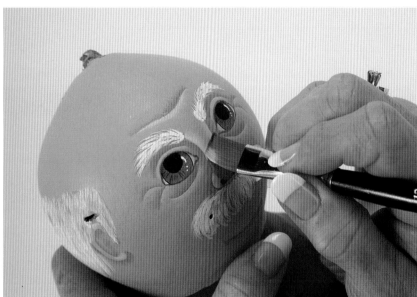

10 Highlight face.

Using the same brush and Santa's Flesh, highlight down each side of the bridge of the nose, the eyebrow, the wrinkles around the eyes, and across the top of the ball of the nose and the nostril covers.

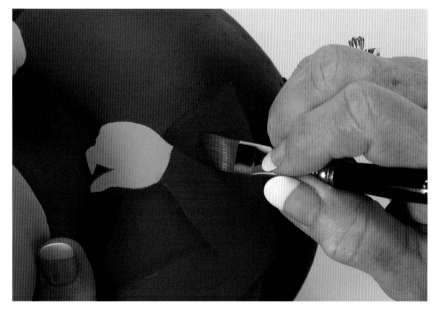

11 Shade the union suit.

Use the shader and Black Cherry to shade the union suit.

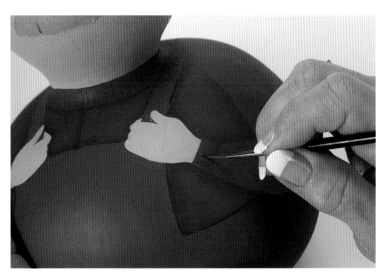

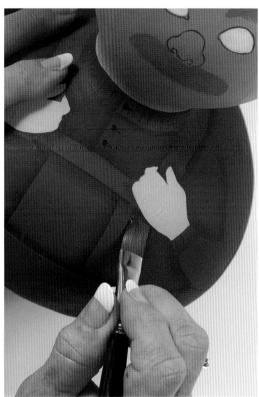

12 Finish the union suit.

Use the liner and thinned Black Cherry to make the lines around the neck and the cuffs of the union suit. The buttons and buttonholes are Candy Bar Brown. All highlighting on the union suit should be done in Fiesta Pink.

13 Shade the coveralls and add stitch details.

Use the shader and Midnight Blue to shade the coveralls. Add stitches in the same color.

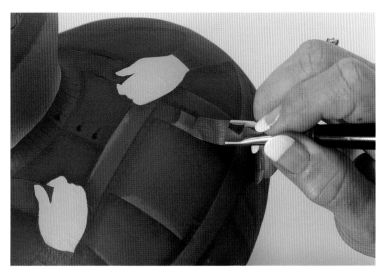

14 Highlight the coveralls.

Use the shader and Tide Pool Blue to highlight the coveralls.

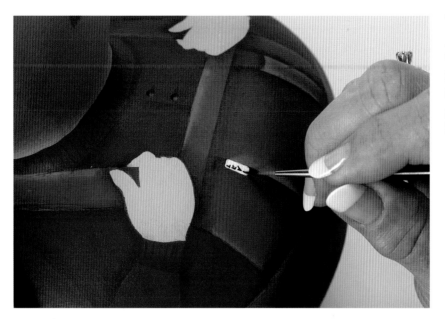

15 Add label and pencil.
Paint in the coverall label with White. Use the liner brush and Black to letter it. Paint in the pencil with Straw and add a Rouge eraser held in place by a Bridgeport Grey metal collar.

16 Shade hands.
Use the shader and Desert Sun Orange to shade the hands.

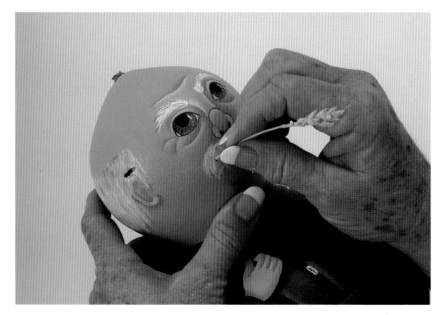

17 Drill holes and add wheat stalk.
Drill holes for the glasses and at the corner of the mustache for the wheat stem. After spraying several light coats of spray finish, place the wheat in the hole.

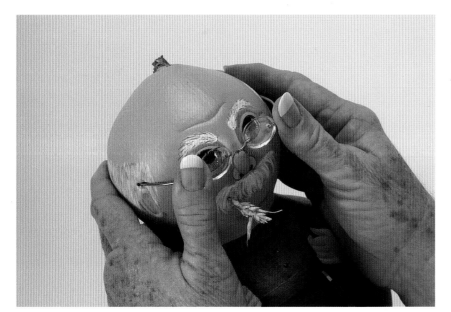

18 Add glasses and hat.
Clip off or straighten the ends of the glasses' earpieces. Place the glasses in the holes you have drilled. Glue the hat in place.

The finished farmer.

frog prince

materials

Delta Ceramcoat acrylics
- 14K Gold
- Black
- Leprechaun
- Pine Green
- Purple
- Sandstone
- White

Loew-Cornell brushes
- Series 7050 10/0 script liner
- Series 7300 nos. 2, 6, 12 flat shaders
- Series 7850 ¼" deerfoot
- Series 7500 ¾" wash brush

Chinese bottle gourd
watercolor paper
craft pick
crown
foamcore board
Delta Ceramcoat Color Float
Delta Waterbased Sealer
Delta Ceramcoat Matte Interior
  Spray Varnish

This little frog is so adorable you'll want to kiss him even if he won't turn into a prince. I used a special technique for painting the eyes that creates that irresistible puppy-dog look. This frog's—I mean prince's—crown also lives a double life as a napkin ring from Crate & Barrel. If you can't locate this napkin ring, a small version of an ornamental gourd called the crown of thorns makes a wonderful substitute.

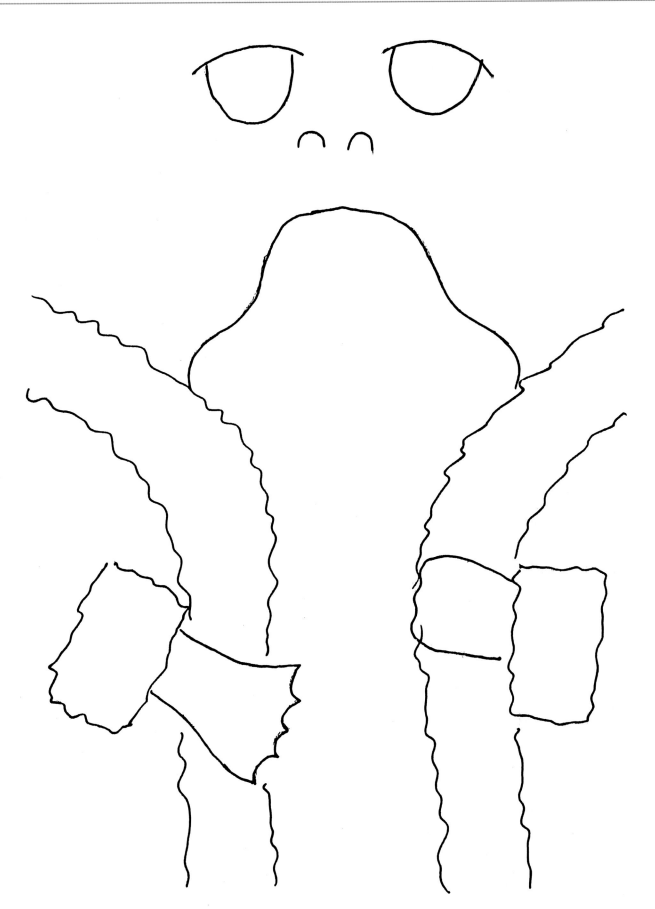

Enlarge this pattern to fit your gourd. Every pattern may require
adjustments to follow the contours of your particular gourd.

Gourd Fun for Everyone

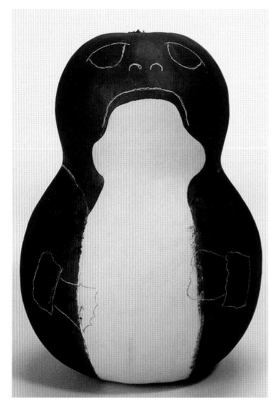
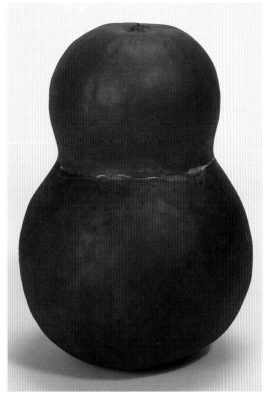

1 Prepare and basecoat the gourd.

Seal gourd with wood sealer. When dry, apply pattern minus details. Basecoat frog Pine Green, stomach Sandstone and robe Purple. Apply rest of pattern and basecoat eyes Black; using a deerfoot, stipple White fur around the edge of the robe.

2 Stipple coat cuffs.

Because the hands cross two colors, basecoat with White before painting Pine Green.

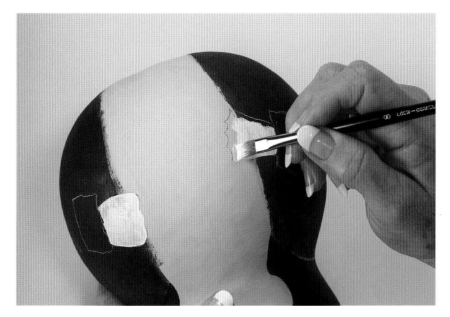

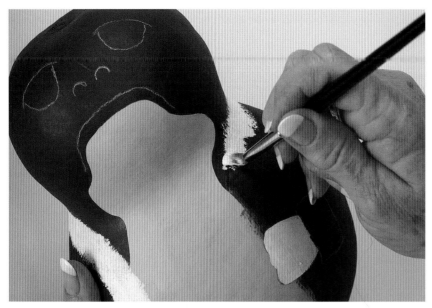

3 Stipple collar.

Use a deerfoot or scruffy brush to stipple in White fur, starting with the cuffs of the coat. Keep the edges shaggy. Continue around the collar.

4 Paint in the hands.

Paint the hands Pine Green over the White basecoating.

5 Add collar details.

Use the 10/0 liner brush and thinned Black to make the ermine tails. Start in the center at the back of the neck and work your way around each side of the robe so that all the tails point downward.

6 Shade nostrils and mouth.

With the hard edge up, fading down, float a shadow of Black inside the nostrils and on the mouth.

7 Highlight eyes, nose and mouth.

With the hard edge down, fading up, use your no. 12 shader to float a highlight of Leprechaun across the tops of the eyes, around the eyes, on top of the nostrils, under the mouth and just below that, on the Sandstone stomach.

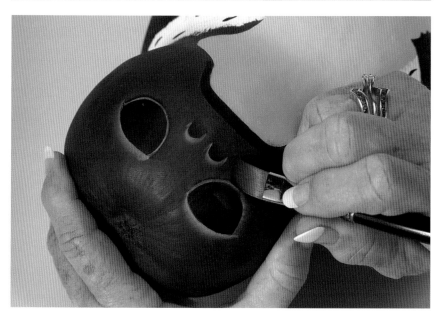

8 Shade under eyes.

After floating a highlight of Leprechaun under each eye fading away from the eye, float a shadow of Black beside it, also fading away. This will leave a soft light-green line under the eyes.

9 Highlight eyeball.
With a no. 12 flat, float a White highlight around the bottom of the eyeball, leaving a thin black border.

10 Add highlights to eyes.
Use the liner brush to place the White comma-stroke highlights in the eyes. The "shine" in the eyes is made with a no. 2 flat.

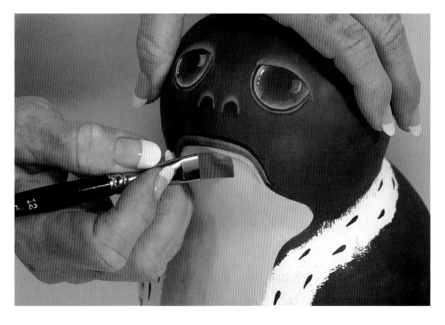

11 Add a shadow under the mouth.
Float a Pine Green shadow under the mouth on the Sandstone, fading down. Spray with several light coats of finish.

12 Add watch and chain.
Use the liner brush and 14K Gold to make the necklace. Glue the watch in place.

13 Make the sign.
Cut a hand from watercolor paper and paint it Pine Green. Don't forget to paint the edges. Cut the sign from foamcore board and letter it in Black. Spray with several light coats of spray finish. Glue a craft pick to the back of the sign. Cut a hand to match the one you painted on the frog out of stiff paper and paint it Pine Green.

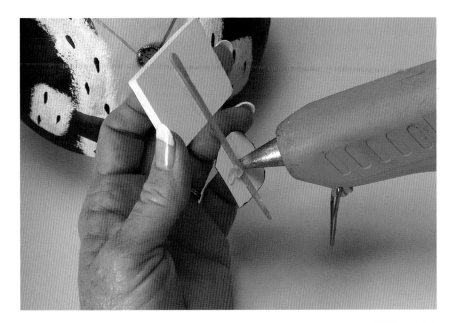

14 Glue the hand to the sign.

15 Glue sign to gourd.
Glue the sign in place, with the paper hand directly overlapping the painted hand on the gourd.

16 **Add the crown.**
Apply glue to the crown and place it on the frog's head.

The finished frog prince.

hobgoblin

materials

Delta Ceramcoat acrylics
- Apple Green
- Bahama Purple
- Black
- Calypso Orange
- Opaque Red
- Tangerine
- White

Loew-Cornell brushes
- Series 7050 10/0 script liner
- Series 7300 no. 12 flat shader
- Series 7500 no. 4 filbert
- Series 7550 ¾" wash brush

coyote gourd
witch hat
silk leaf
two 6"-long, ¼"-diameter or
  larger wooden dowels
glue gun
drill
saw for cutting feet
½"-thick wood for feet
Delta Ceramcoat Color Float
Delta Waterbased Sealer
Delta Ceramcoat Satin Interior
  Spray Varnish

I love the Redball sneakers on this little Halloween harbinger. He isn't difficult to make. Just exercise caution when drilling the holes for his legs: Coyote gourds are very thin-shelled and fragile. If cracks develop, they can be repaired with wood glue. You can cut out this little guy's sneakers with a coping saw or jig saw, but I find the bandsaw to be the easiest to use.

Enlarge this pattern to fit your gourd. Every pattern may require adjustments to follow the contours of your particular gourd.

1 Prepare gourd and paint pumpkin background.

Drill holes in the bottom of the gourd for the legs. Seal gourd and let dry. Use ¾" wash brush and Calypso Orange to basecoat entire gourd. Apply pattern. Float Tangerine lines from top to bottom for pumpkin sections. Use the no. 12 shader and Tangerine to float the sections of the pumpkin.

2 Draw the face.
Use a charcoal pencil or transfer paper to draw the pattern on.

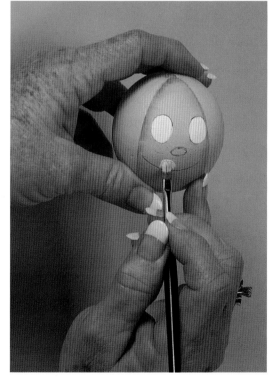

3 Basecoat eyes and tooth.
Using a small filbert and White, basecoat the tooth and eyes. This will require at least two coats for solid coverage.

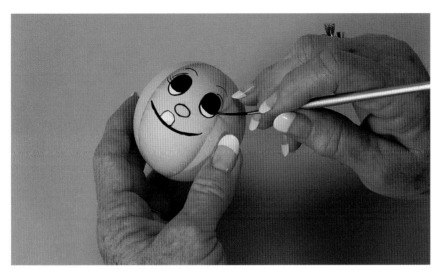

4 Finish eyes and mouth.
Use the filbert to fill in the irises with Black. Use the 10/0 liner and thinned Black to make the eyebrows, eyelashes and mouth. Use the same brush and thinned White to put the sparkle in the eyes.

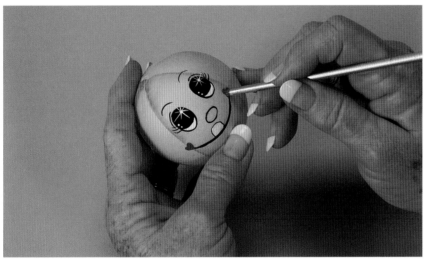

5 Add heart details.
Use the brush handle to place two equal dots of Opaque Red side by side. Pull a "V" between them to join them. This is a Dolly Parton heart.

6 Finish hobgoblin.
Cut feet from ½"-thick wood according to the pattern. Drill holes in shoes and glue in dowels. Paint dowels Tangerine with Bahama Purple stripes. Shoe soles are White, tops are Black, laces are Apple Green and balls on the sides are Opaque Red. Spray with several coats of spray finish. Glue hat and leaf in place.

snowman

materials

Delta Ceramcoat acrylics
- Black
- Calypso Orange
- Persimmon
- Tangerine
- White

Loew-Cornell brushes
- Series 7050 10/0 script liner
- Series 7850 ¼" deerfoot
- Series 7300 nos. 2, 6, 12
  flat shaders
- Series 7500 ¾" mop brush

Chinese bottle gourd
glue gun
short piece of ¼" dowel for nose
small top hat
small scarf
two mushroom birds
twigs for arms
file or belt sander
drill
Delta Waterbased Sealer
Delta Ceramcoat Color Float
Delta Ceramcoat Satin Interior
  Spray Varnish

Now here's a little fellow who's ready for whatever winter brings! He's made from a Chinese bottle gourd, and his carrot nose is formed from a dowel. To get the point (no pun intended), I sharpened the dowel with a pencil sharpener before I cut the length needed for the nose. Don't sharpen it too much! You can also shape the nose with a sander, but I find my method to be much faster.

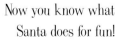

Now you know what
Santa does for fun!

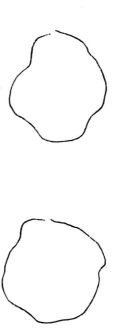

Enlarge this pattern to fit your gourd. Every pattern may require
adjustments to follow the contours of your particular gourd.

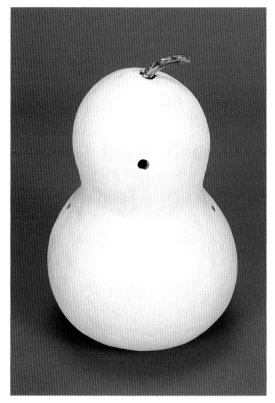

1 Basecoat gourd and shape nose.
Seal the gourd and basecoat in White. Prepare the carrot nose by sharpening the dowel in a pencil sharpener and then using a file or the edge of a belt sander to make grooves along the sides.

2 Drill holes for nose and arms.
Drill a hole for the nose and check to make sure the dowel will fit. Drill holes for the twig arms as well.

3 Transfer the pattern.
After the basecoat is dry, use a charcoal pencil (or transfer paper) to draw the pattern on.

4 Create facial features.

Use the 10/0 liner and thinned black paint for the eyelashes, eyebrows and mouth. Float White over the Black at bottom of eyes. Add glints on the coal buttons with White.

5 Add sparkle to eyes.

Use the 10/0 liner and thinned White to place the sparkle in the eyes.

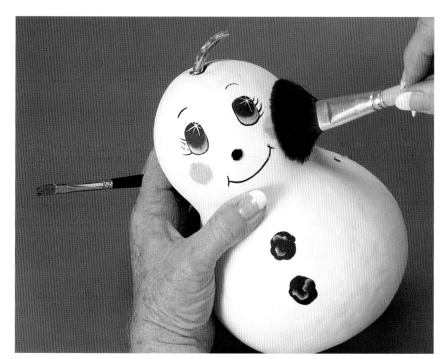

6 Paint cheeks and nose.

Moisten the cheek area. Lightly dab Persimmon in a circle with a deerfoot brush or a damp cotton swab. Before it can dry, gently mop with the mop brush to soften the effect. You may not get this right the first time (I don't always), but if it doesn't look right, just wipe it off and try again. Now paint the nose Calypso Orange, shade with Tangerine and glue into place. Spray with several light coats of spray finish.

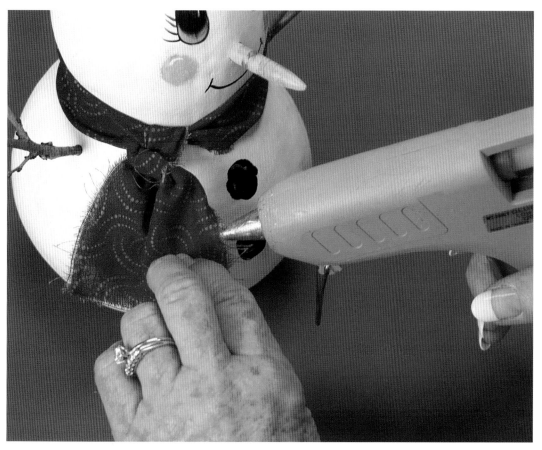

7 Add accessories.

After you have glued the twig arms in place, tie the scarf around the snowman's neck and glue the ends in place.

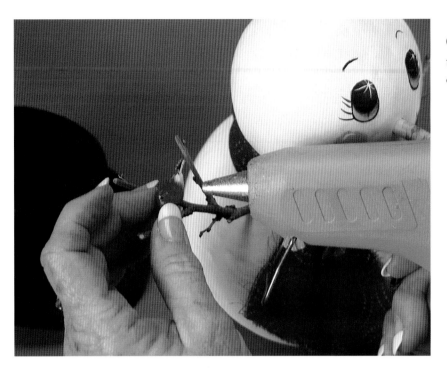

8 Add birds.
Glue a mushroom bird on one of the arms and another bird on the hat crown.

9 Add hat.
Glue the hat in place and enjoy your snowman.

The finished snowman.

toboggan kid ornament

materials

Delta Ceramcoat acrylics
- Black
- Desert Sun Orange
- Medium Flesh
- Rouge
- White

Loew-Cornell brushes
- Series 7050 10/0 script liner
- Series 7300 no. 12 flat shader

egg gourd
child's sock for hat
strong thread
glue gun
6" length of ribbon for hanging
pom-pom for hat
Delta Ceramcoat Color Float
Delta Waterbased Sealer
Delta Ceramcoat Matte Interior
  Spray Varnish

Here's another egg gourd ornament in the form of an impish winter sledder with a sock hat cocked over one eye. You can make lots of these little ornaments in no time—for yourself and for gift-giving. If you don't want to take the time to make a hat from a sock, you can paint the hat on and just glue the pom-pom on top. If you paint the hat, there is no limit to the wonderful patterns you can add to it—trees, reindeer, snowflakes, school letters—just let your imagination run wild!

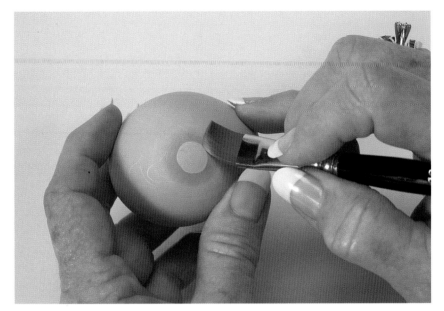

1 Basecoat gourd and paint nose.

After basecoating the gourd in Medium Flesh, float Desert Sun Orange in a circle for the nose.

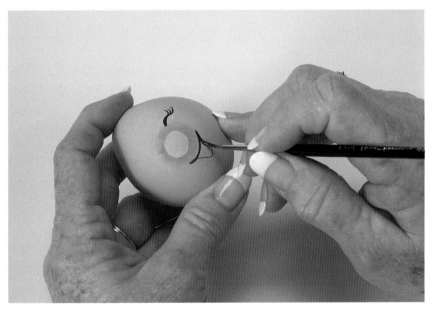

2 Outline eye and mouth.

Use the liner brush and Black to make the eye and mouth outlines.

3 Paint cheeks.

Float Rouge across the cheek and the top of the nose with the no. 12 flat shader.

4 Add shine on nose.
Use White and the liner brush to apply a comma stroke on the nose for shine. Spray with several light coats of spray finish.

5 Make sock hat.
With the right side out, tie a strong thread around a child's sock about 3" down from the top and touch a little hot glue to the knot. Cut the toe off.

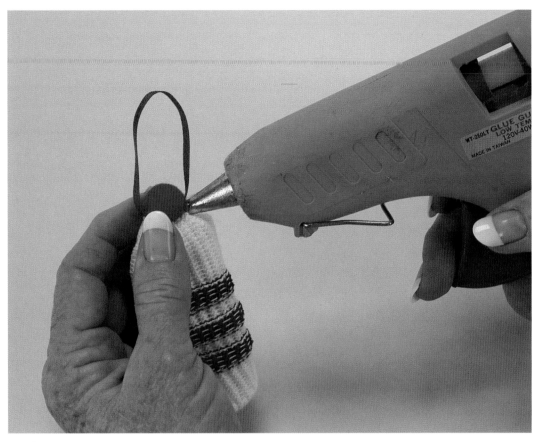

6 Add ribbon hanger and pom-pom.

Turn the sock wrong side out and glue a loop of ribbon on for a hanger. Glue a pom-pom inside the loop.

7 Turn the cuff up.

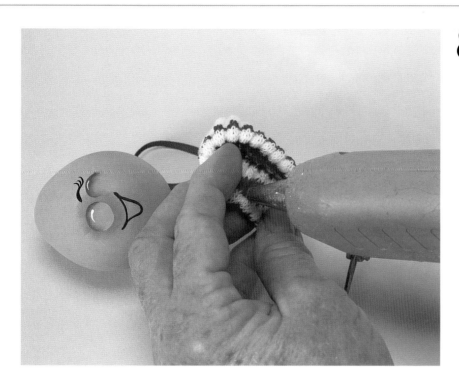

8 Glue the hat in place.

The finished ornament.

toy soldier

materials

Delta Ceramcoat acrylics
- 14K Gold
- Black
- Black Cherry
- Blueberry
- Bridgeport Grey
- Caucasian Flesh
- Medium Flesh
- Opaque Red
- Rouge
- Spice Brown
- White

Loew-Cornell brushes
- Series 7050 10/0 script liner
- Series 7300 no. 12 flat shader
- Series 7520 ½" filbert rake

small bat gourd
white pompon
furniture button
drill
masking tape
glue gun
Delta Ceramcoat Color Float
Delta Waterbased Sealer
Delta Ceramcoat Matte Interior
  Spray Varnish

This soldier looks so proper you almost take him seriously—until you see his little button nose. Shading easily produces all the details on the tunic, and gold paint adds buttons and braid.

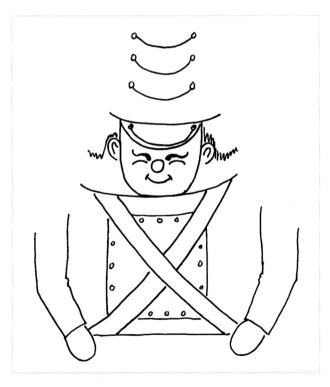

Enlarge this pattern to fit your gourd. Every pattern may require adjustments to follow the contours of your particular gourd.

1 Basecoat gourd.

Seal the gourd with the wood sealer and allow to dry. Apply pattern minus features and details. Basecoat hat and pants Blueberry, the tunic Opaque Red and hands and face Medium Flesh. The hair is Spice Brown, with individual hairs suggested by using a rake brush.

 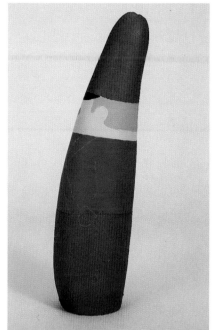

2 Fit the nose.

Drill hole for nose and check the furniture button for fit. You can also do this step before you basecoat—that way you won't ruin your basecoat if you have to adjust the fit.

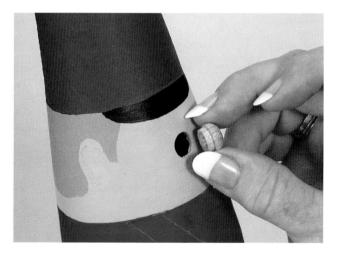

3 Start painting the face.

Apply pattern details. Float Caucasian Flesh under the hat brim, around ears and at sleeve edges. Shade inside the ears with Desert Sun.

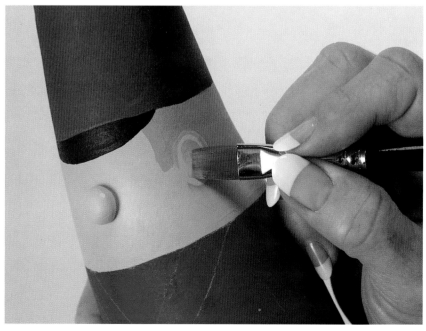

4 Outline features.

Use the 10/0 liner and thinned Black for the eyes, mouth and chin strap.

5 Paint the cheeks.

Use the no. 12 flat shader to float C-stroke Rouge cheeks.

6 Paint straps and shade tunic.

Tape off cross on chest and paint White. Use the no.12 flat shader and Black Cherry to shade the tunic around the shirt front and on each side of the arms.

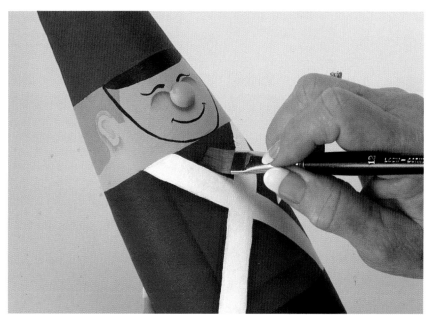

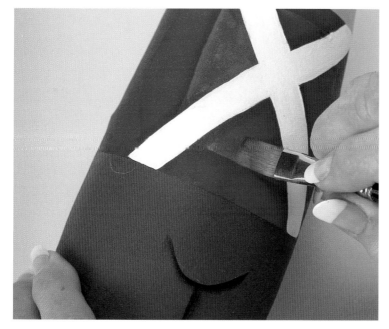

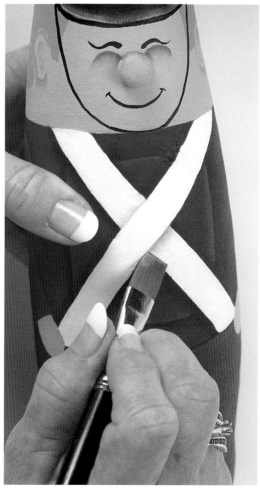

7 Highlight tunic.
Highlight the tunic with a float of Tangerine.

8 Shade straps.
Shade with Bridgeport Grey where the straps cross each other.

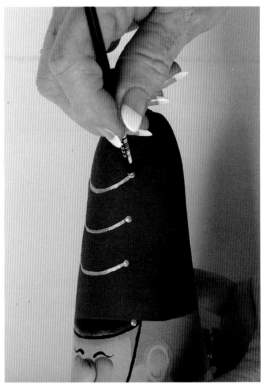

9 Add braid to hat.
Use 14K Gold and the 10/0 liner brush to make the braid on the hat.

10 Add buttons to hat.
Use the brush handle to make the buttons on the hat.

11 Add buttons to tunic.
Use the brush handle to make the buttons on the tunic.

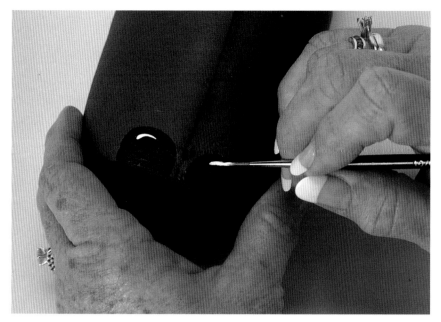

12 Shine the shoes.
Pull White comma strokes on the shoes for shine.

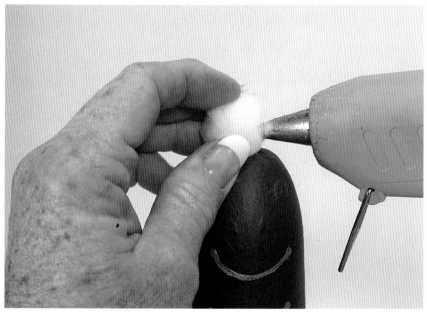

13 Finish hat.
After spraying on several light coats of finish, glue the pom-pom on top of the hat.

The finished soldier.

part two

Gallery

I have offered general instructions for painting the gourds in this section—if you have painted some of the gourds in the first section, you know all you need to know to paint these projects. Get creative! Adapt designs to the gourds you choose. The best part about painting gourds is letting the particular shape of your gourd inspire you. The projects in this section should give you plenty of ideas.

materials

Delta Ceramcoat acrylics

- 14K Gold
- Black
- Black Cherry
- Bridgeport Grey
- Burnt Sienna
- Calypso Orange
- Caucasian Flesh
- Dark Brown
- Denim Blue
- Green Sea
- Medium Flesh
- Opaque Red
- Persimmon
- Pine Green
- Rouge
- Santa's Flesh
- Tangerine
- White

Loew-Cornell brushes

- Series 7050 10/0 script liner
- Series 7300 nos. 4, 12 flat shaders
- Series 7550 ¾" wash brush

12"-tall club gourd
witch hat
small broom
curly doll hair
glue gun
watercolor paper
Delta Ceramcoat Color Float
Delta Waterbased Sealer
Delta Ceramcoat Satin Interior
  Spray Varnish

apple witch

BASECOAT
Seal gourd and let dry. Apply pattern minus facial details. Basecoat hands and face in Medium Flesh, pumpkin in Calypso Orange, leaves in Green Sea, apple in Opaque Red, dress in Black.

FACE, LIPS AND HANDS
Apply face pattern, and outline features with Burnt Sienna. Her lips and fingernails are Persimmon. Shade hands with Caucasian Flesh. Fill eyes in solid with White. Shade the wrinkles with Caucasian Flesh and highlight with Santa's Flesh. Float Rouge heavily across cheeks, fading up. Shade upper lip with Black Cherry. The iris is Denim Blue, the pupil is Black. Place White highlight in the eyes. Glasses are 14K Gold. The "shine" is made with your liner brush and White.

Don't hand out apples if you have this wicked witch greet trick-or-treaters at your door! If you're a Wizard of Oz fan, place Dorothy's little dog in the witch's hands instead of the apple and change the sign to include an appropriate message.

"What bird?"

DRESS

Float Bridgeport Grey around the edges of collar and sleeves. Use the liner brush and thinned Bridgeport Grey for fine lines.

APPLE AND PUMPKIN

Shade apple with Black Cherry. Leaves have Pine Green veins; stem is Dark Brown. Shade the pumpkin with Tangerine and fill in features with Black. Line the edge of the openings with Black Cherry. The sparkles are made with your stylus and White; pull lines from the center of each sparkle with your liner.

FINISH

When dry, glue hair, hat and broom in place. Make the sign from watercolor paper and glue to the hat. Spray with several light coats of spray finish.

Here's a great centerpiece, but don't try to carve this bird!

Enlarge this pattern to fit your gourd. Every
pattern may require adjustments to follow
the contours of your particular gourd.

Maybe the sky is falling. Maybe it ain't. This poultry person looks a little too laid back to be very worried about it. You will want a whole flock of these cluckers in various colors for your collection. You don't have to be a sculptor to make the extra parts for this project! Just play around with the clay and have fun.

chicken little

materials

Delta Ceramcoat acrylics
- Georgia Clay
- Pigskin
- Straw
- Tomato Spice
- White

Loew-Cornell brushes
- Series 7050 10/0 script liner
- Series 7300 no. 12 flat shader
- Series 7550 ¾" wash brush

large egg gourd
FIMO clay
florist wire
florist tape
Delta Ceramcoat Color Float
small beads
Delta Waterbased Sealer
Delta Ceramcoat Satin Interior
  Spray Varnish

WINGS, BEAK AND COMB
Mold the comb, wings and beak from FIMO clay. Make two small balls of clay and press onto the egg for eyes. Press a small green bead into each eye for the iris. Bake according to package directions while attached to the gourd. When cool, check to see if the pieces are still firmly attached. If not, glue them. Drill holes for feet and glue them in place.

BODY
Seal the gourd then basecoat in Pigskin. Make Georgia Clay C-strokes all over the chicken using the no. 12 shader. Float a shade along the bottom of the wings. Paint the comb Tomato Spice and the beak and feet Straw. Paint the eyes White, leaving the green beads showing. Finish with several light coats of spray finish.

Chicken Feet

1 Cut a piece of florist wire into four equal pieces and wrap with florist tape. Wrap the four pieces together for about half of the length.

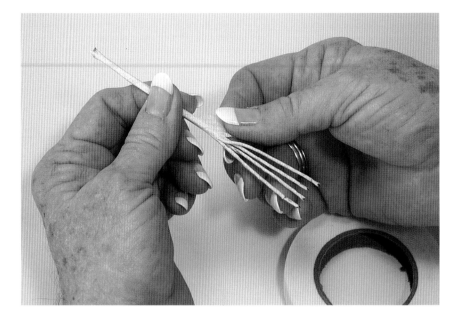

2 Spread the toes so that three point forward and one points backward.

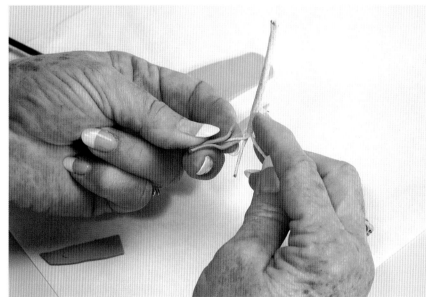

3 If you have a pasta machine, run the conditioned clay through it to make it very thin. If you don't have a machine, roll it out using a paint bottle as shown.

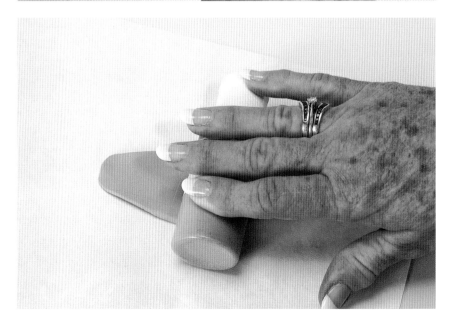

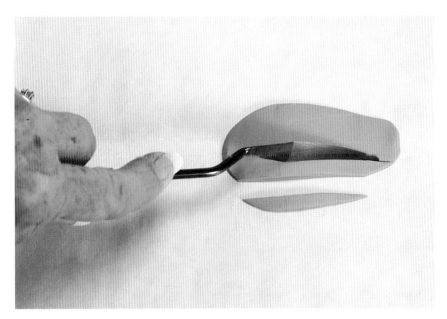

4 Cut the flattened clay into narrow strips the length of the toes and legs.

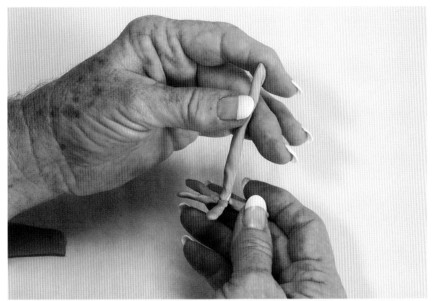

5 Wrap the individual wires with clay strips until no wire shows. Check to be sure all toes are covered and in the correct position so the feet will stand.

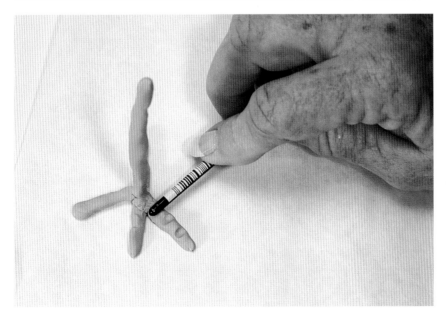

6 Use a small brush handle to make indentions in the toes as shown. Bake the feet according to package instructions. When cool, paint with Straw to match the beak.

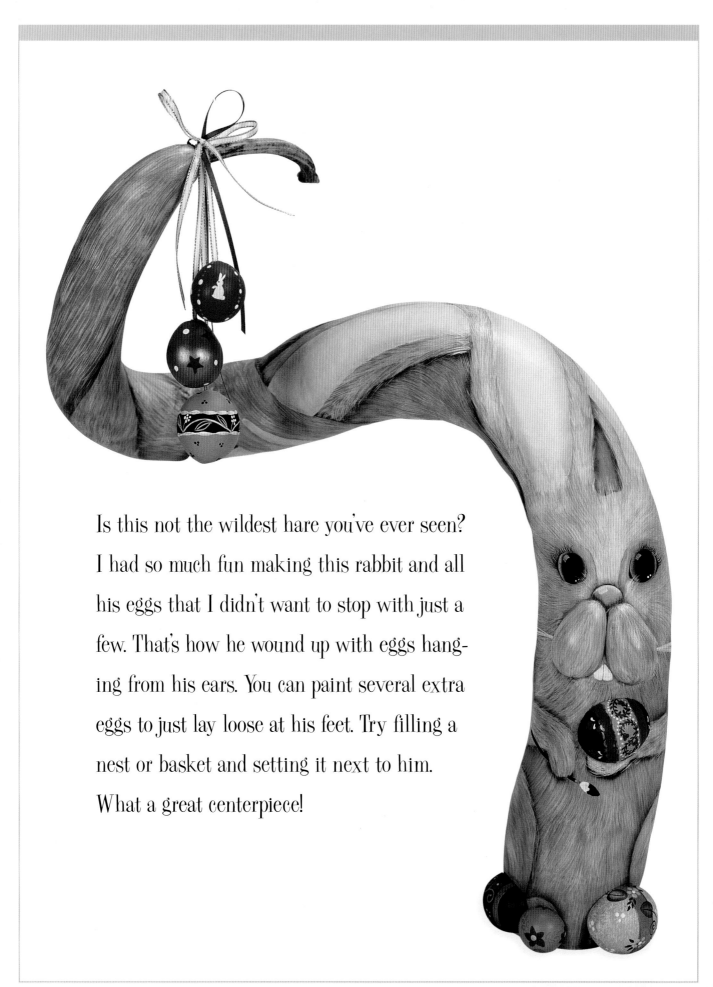

Is this not the wildest hare you've ever seen? I had so much fun making this rabbit and all his eggs that I didn't want to stop with just a few. That's how he wound up with eggs hanging from his ears. You can paint several extra eggs to just lay loose at his feet. Try filling a nest or basket and setting it next to him. What a great centerpiece!

easter rabbit

materials

Delta Ceramcoat acrylics
- 14K Gold
- Avalon Blue
- Bahama Purple
- Black
- Bridgeport Grey
- Charcoal
- Denim Blue
- Nectar Coral
- Persimmon
- Rose Petal Pink
- White

Loew-Cornell brushes
- Series 7050 10/0 script liner
- Series 7300 nos. 4, 12 flat shaders
- Series 7520 ½" filbert rake
- Series 7550 1" wash brush

snake gourd
craft whiskers
egg gourds
Delta Waterbased Sealer
ribbon
glue gun
Delta Color Float
Delta Ceramcoat Satin Interior Spray Varnish

BASECOAT
Seal the gourds. Paint the entire snake gourd Bridgeport Grey. Basecoat one egg Avalon Blue, one Persimmon and one Bahama Purple.

FACE AND BODY
Apply pattern and paint nose and inside ears Rose Petal Pink. Shade with Nectar Coral. Float Charcoal around ears, under cheeks and around arms and legs. Use a rake brush and White to make the fur. Paint teeth White, eyes and eyelashes Black. Pull a few stray hairs of White up from the nose into the eyes. Float White in the eyes and add highlights.

ACCESSORIES
Paint the brush tip and the egg the bunny is holding Denim Blue. Paint bunnies and stripes White. Comma stroke design and brush ferrule are 14K Gold. Spray with several light coats of satin spray finish.

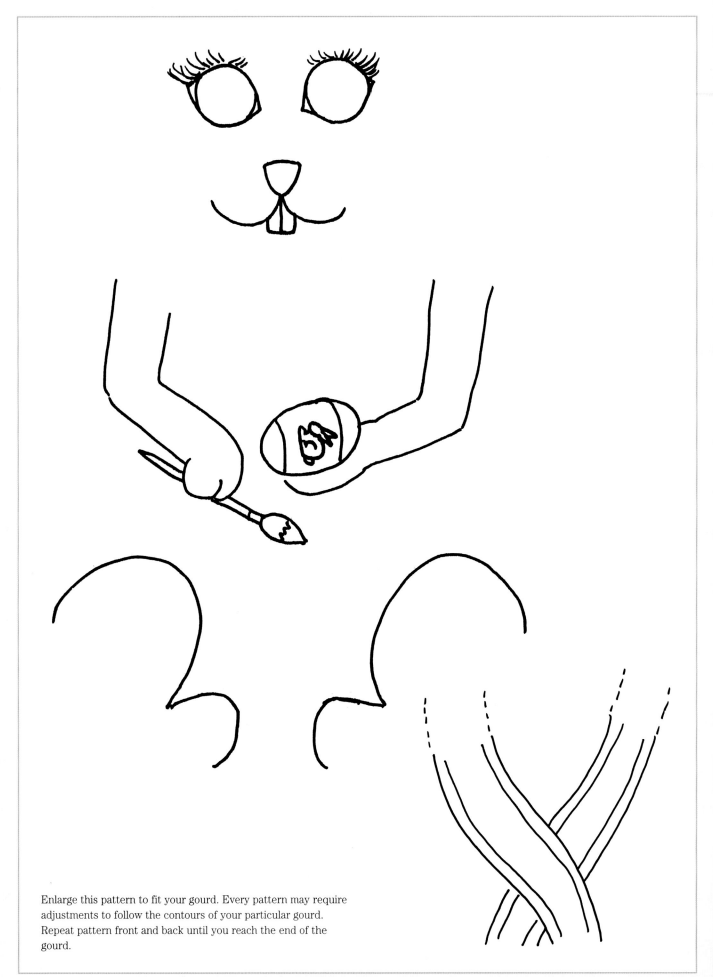

Enlarge this pattern to fit your gourd. Every pattern may require adjustments to follow the contours of your particular gourd. Repeat pattern front and back until you reach the end of the gourd.

WHISKERS AND EGG ORNAMENTS

Drill small holes for the whiskers and glue in place. Glue various lengths of craft ribbon to the eggs and glue the other ends to the stem of the snake gourd. Glue a bow where the ribbons meet the gourd stem.

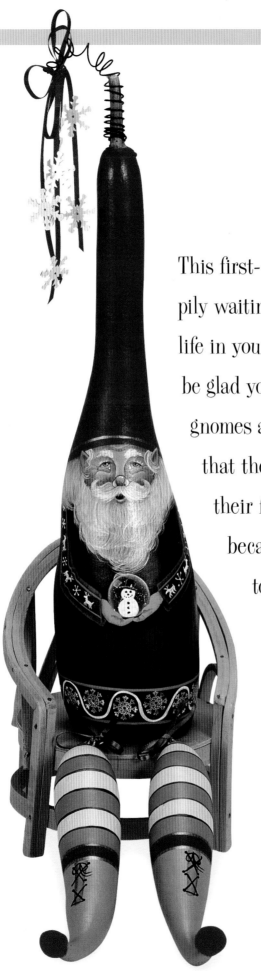

This first-class Santa's helper is happily waiting for you to bring him to life in your home. I'm sure you will be glad you did. Did you know that gnomes always wear red hats? And that the reason you never see their footprints in your garden is because the treads on the bottoms of their boots look like a bird's foot? Now you know what to look for!

gnome shelfsitter

BASECOAT

Seal gourds and let dry. Apply pattern minus details. Basecoat boots Lichen Grey, tunic Mallard Green, hat Opaque Red, flesh Medium Flesh, legs West Sunset Yellow. Basecoat hair and beard Bridgeport Grey, keeping the edges feathery.

FACE AND HAIR

Apply facial features and outline with Burnt Sienna. Highlight features and hands with Santa's Flesh, shade with Desert Sun Orange. Float Rouge across cheeks and bottom of nose from ear to ear, fading up. Mop to soften if needed. Fill in nostrils and mouth with Cinnamon. Fill eye in solid with White. The iris is Blue Heaven, the pupil Black. Place a highlight with White. Use the filbert rake and thinned White for hair and beard, use 10/0 liner for eyelashes, eyebrows, mustache and little stray hairs. Paint a thin 14K Gold line around the bottom of the hat about ¼" up from the bottom edge.

materials

Delta Ceramcoat acrylics
- 14K Gold
- Black
- Blue Heaven
- Bridgeport Grey
- Burnt Sienna
- Cinnamon
- Desert Sun Orange
- Hammered Iron
- Heritage Green
- Laguna Blue
- Lichen Grey
- Mallard Green
- Medium Flesh
- Opaque Red
- Rouge
- Santa's Flesh
- West Sunset Yellow
- White

Loew-Cornell brushes
- Series 7050 10/0 script liner
- Series 7300 no. 12 flat shader
- Series 7520 ½" filbert rake
- Series 7550 ¾" wash brush
- no. 32 fan
- no. 275 mop

14" bat gourd
two 7" banana gourds
snowflake sequins
snowflake stamp
red pom-poms
craft wire, 19 gauge
ribbon
small eye screws
Delta Waterbased Sealer
Delta Color Float
Delta Ceramcoat Satin Interior
 Spray Varnish

Tunic and Snow Globe

Float shadows on tunic with a mix of Black and Mallard 1:3 and highlight with Laguna Blue. I use a coin to make the snow globe circle. Float White around the circle, fading toward the center. Basecoat the snowman in White. Basecoat hat and features Black. Spatter snow with a fan brush and thinned White, wiping any stray spatters off immediately. (I used a template for a mask.)

Thin lines on tunic bottom and sleeves are Heritage Green. Snowflakes and reindeer are White. The snowflakes on tunic are done with a rubber stamp and thinned White. Brush paint across stamp and blot excess off on a paper towel before stamping. Rock stamp slightly to allow for curve of the gourd.

Legs and Feet

Apply Heritage Green stripes to legs using a no. 12 flat, then add Mallard Green stripes on each side of first stripe using liner brush. Apply Opaque Red stripes to top of boots and a narrow Gold band on each side of the red stripe. Float shading for boot tongues with Hammered Iron. Laces are Black.

Finishing

Spray with several light coats of spray finish. When dry, screw eye screws into the base of elf and tops of legs. Be sure to allow enough room between legs. Attach the legs by looping ribbon through the eye screws. Hot glue pom-poms on toes of boots. Coil craft wire around a pencil or brush handle, then slip over gourd stem. Bend wire over and tie ribbons to the end. Hot glue snowflake sequins to ribbons.

This little guy doesn't know that all gnomes are supposed to wear red hats.

Would you like to sit on Santa's lap?

Enlarge this pattern to fit your gourd. Every pattern may require
adjustments to follow the contours of your particular gourd.
These snowflakes are made with a rubber stamp and thinned
White. Because of the curved surface, you must slightly roll the
stamp to get a good, even image. This doesn't always work the
first time, so be prepared to wipe it off once or twice.

I take my ideas where I find them, and sometimes that can be in the most unexpected places. I recently visited the third-grade class at Lake Hamilton Elementary. We spent a day painting egg gourds together, and at the end of the day a little fellow named Bradley Gaines came to me with a sketch. "Why don't you paint one like this?" he asked, showing me a drawing of a hamburger. You can see here the results of that meeting.

hamburger

materials

Delta Ceramcoat acrylics
- Avocado
- Black Cherry
- Black Green
- Boston Fern
- Burnt Umber
- Cactus Green
- Chrome Green Light
- Dark Burnt Umber
- Light Ivory
- Old Parchment
- Olive Yellow
- Raw Sienna
- Spice Brown
- Spice Tan
- Tomato Spice
- Wedgewood Green
- West Sunset Yellow
- White
- Wild Rose

Loew-Cornell brushes
- Series 7350 10/0 liner
- Series 7300 nos. 6, 12 flat shaders
- Series 7150 ¾" wash brush

canteen gourd
Delta Waterbased Sealer
white chalk pencil
Delta Ceramcoat Satin Interior
  Spray Varnish

BASECOAT

Seal gourd and allow to dry. Use the ¾" wash brush to basecoat the entire gourd in Spice Tan. Hold a chalk pencil against the gourd and rotate, scribing a line around it about one third of the way up from the bottom. Apply pattern above this line.

BUN, MEAT AND SESAME SEEDS

Stipple Raw Sienna around the gourd. While wet, stipple Burnt Umber to make the meat pattie. Drop down about ½" and float a line of Spice Brown with the no. 12 shader, fading up. Add vertical floated lines all around between this line and the meat. Float random rippling lines of Spice Brown on the top and bottom of the bun. Highlight these lines with Spice Tan and White 1:1. The sesame seeds are the same mix. Shade beside each seed with Spice Brown and highlight with West Sunset Yellow.

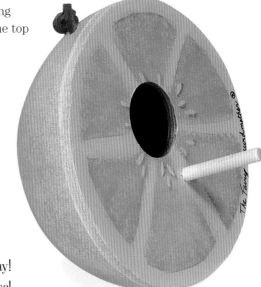

Make a bird happy today!
Paint a gourd birdhouse!

VEGGIES AND CONDIMENTS

Use the no. 6 flat and Light Ivory to create onion slices. Shade with Old Parchment. Pickles are Boston Fern shaded with Black Green and highlighted with a flip float of Olive Yellow. Tomatoes are Tomato Spice shaded with Black Cherry and highlighted with a flip float of Wild Rose. Lettuce is Cactus Green, shaded with Chrome Green Light, then Avocado (to darken the shading in places). Use the liner and thinned Wedgewood Green to make the veins. Glaze the lettuce with Avocado. Fill in the crevices between the veggies with Dark Burnt Umber. Float a line of Spice Brown fading up around the bun above the lettuce.

Finish with several light coats of satin spray finish.

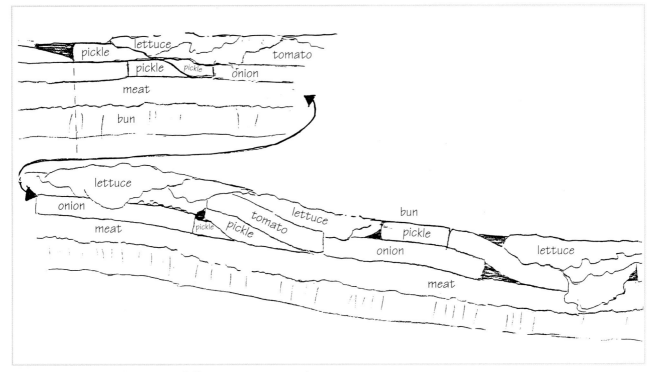

Enlarge this pattern to fit your gourd. Every pattern may require adjustments to follow the contours of your particular gourd.

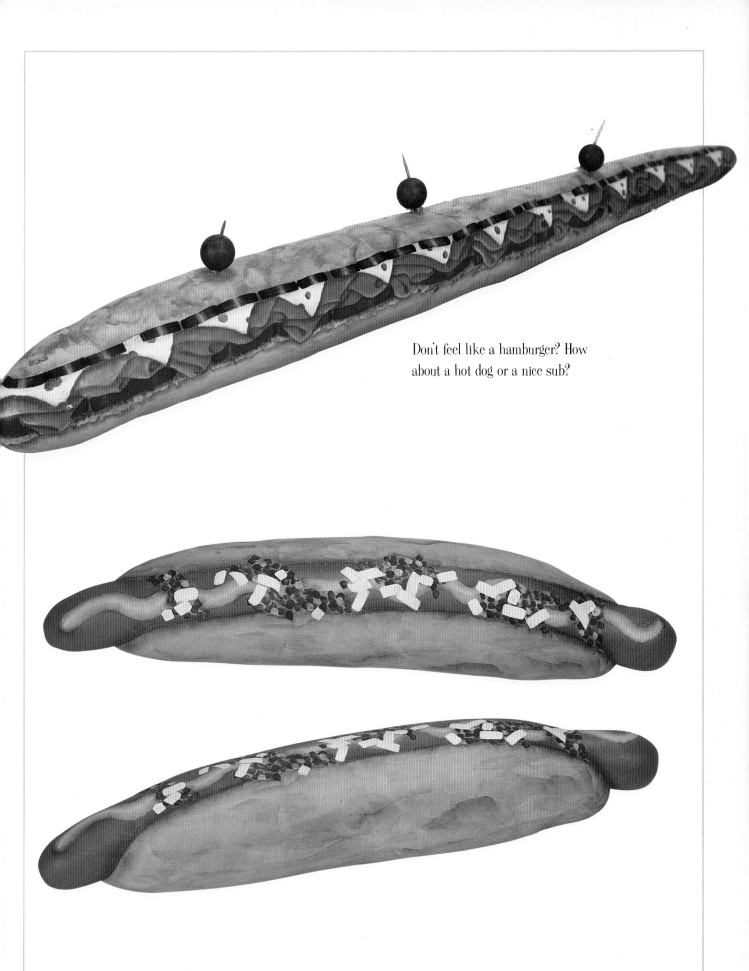

Don't feel like a hamburger? How about a hot dog or a nice sub?

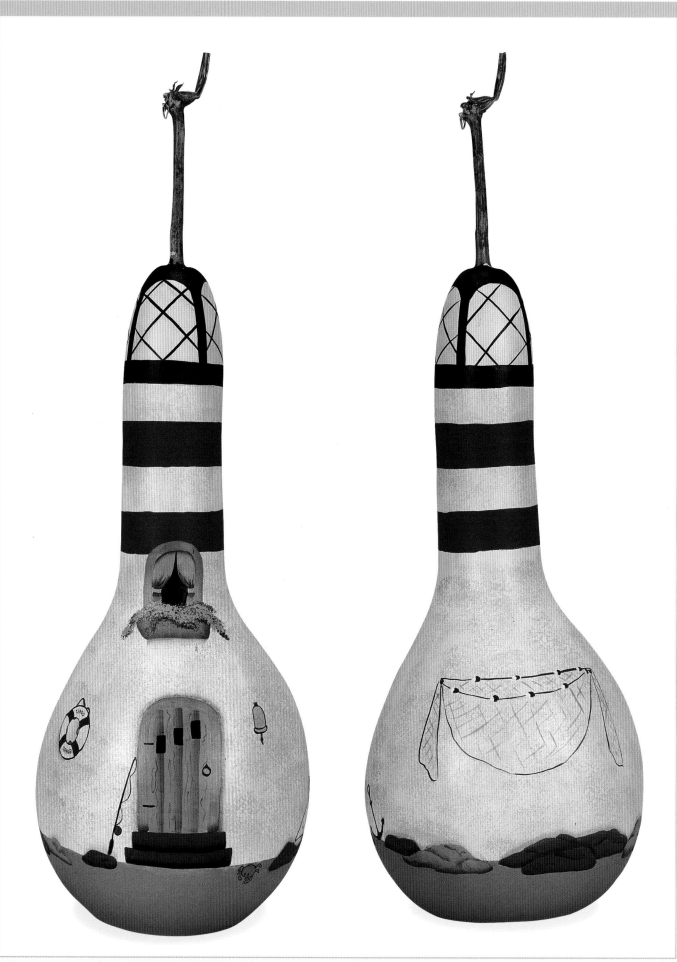

Gourd Fun for Everyone

lighthouse

I am amazed at how many lighthouse collectors there are out there. Perhaps you know someone who would enjoy receiving this as a gift. This one is pretty generic, but you can change the stripes and other decorations to match your favorite real lighthouse. You could also add seagulls or seashells. Use your imagination and make the lighthouse yours.

materials

Delta Ceramcoat acrylics
- Black
- Butter Yellow
- Custard
- Forest Green
- Hippo Grey
- Nectar Coral
- Nightfall Blue
- Opaque Red
- Pigskin
- Quaker Grey
- Territorial Beige
- Trail Tan
- Wedgewood Blue
- Wedgewood Green
- White

Loew-Cornell brushes
- Series 7050 10/0 script liner
- Series 7300 no. 12 flat shader
- Series 7850 ¼" deerfoot
- Series 7550 ¾" wash brush

dipper gourd
sponge
Delta Waterbased Sealer
Delta Color Float
Delta Ceramcoat Matte Interior
  Spray Varnish

BASECOAT
Seal gourd and when dry, basecoat White. Sponge Quaker Grey all over the top portion and Trail Tan on the bottom. Apply pattern. I find it is much easier to apply a pattern to a round object if I first cut the pattern apart and then place the various features where needed.

LIGHTHOUSE
Basecoat the door Trail Tan. Float lines down the door with Territorial Beige. The window and door frames are Wedgewood Green. Basecoat inside the windows Black with Wedgewood Blue curtains. The steps are Hippo Grey, shaded with Black. The bell is Butter Yellow.

You can either measure or eyeball the stripes. I used a ¾" brush to make the Opaque Red stripes.

LIGHT TOWER
Measure down from the top of the gourd about 3" and paint a Black band around it. Divide the top vertically into four equal parts and separate with bands of Black. Fill in with Custard and line with Black for the windowpanes.

ACCESSORIES

The crab is Wedgewood Green. The anchor is Hippo Grey shaded with Black. The pelican's bill and feet are Pigskin. The rocks are various browns and grays taken from the palette. Shade behind them with Quaker Grey if you like. Stipple Forest Green with the deerfoot in the windowbox, and repeat with Nectar Coral for the flowers. Shade the curtains with Nightfall Blue. The fishing rod is Black; the reel and line are Hippo Grey. The life preserver is White and Opaque Red with Pigskin rope. The fishing net is outlined with Hippo Grey; the cross-hatching is Quaker Grey. The floats are White and Opaque Red. Outline the bell, preserver, pelican and crab with Black. Finish with several light coats of finish.

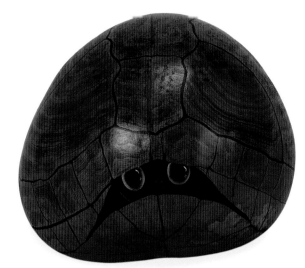

This chap doesn't need a lighthouse. He always has a place to stay.

Coast Gourd

Continue rocks by repeating.

Enlarge this pattern to fit your gourd. Every pattern may require adjustments to follow the contours of your particular gourd.

Gourd Fun for Everyone

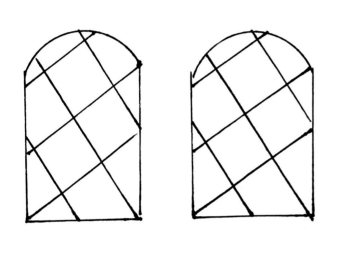

Adjust top by quartering top of gourd to make windows fit.

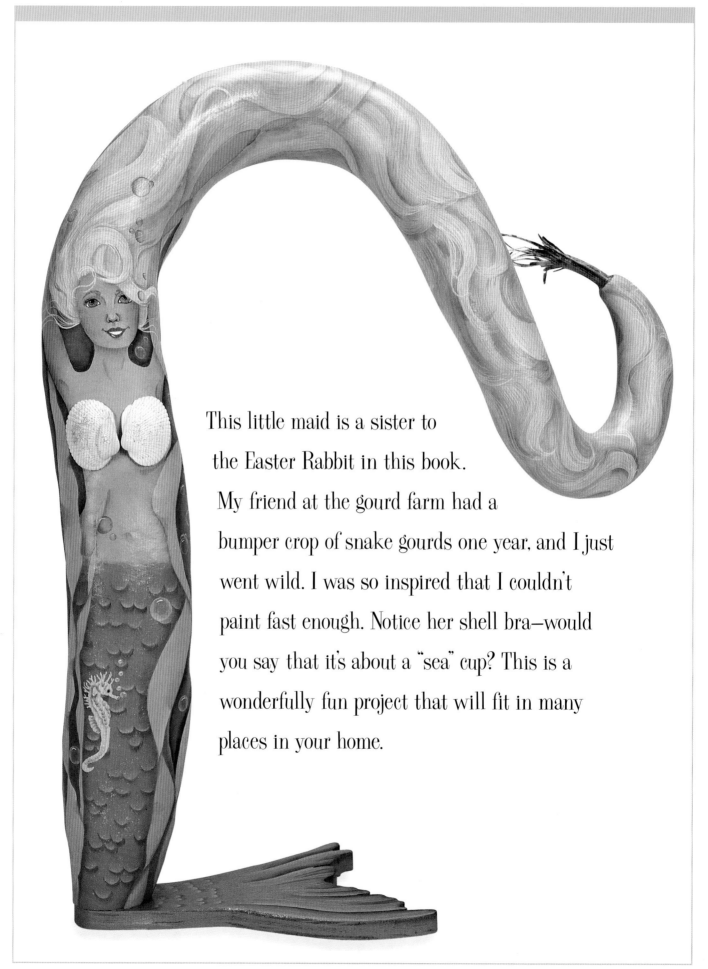

This little maid is a sister to the Easter Rabbit in this book. My friend at the gourd farm had a bumper crop of snake gourds one year, and I just went wild. I was so inspired that I couldn't paint fast enough. Notice her shell bra—would you say that it's about a "sea" cup? This is a wonderfully fun project that will fit in many places in your home.

muriel
the mermaid

materials

Delta Ceramcoat acrylics
- Alpine Green
- Antique Gold
- Black
- Chrome Green Light
- Cloudberry Tan
- Custard
- Dark Flesh
- Dark Forest Green
- Desert Sun Orange
- Dunes Beige
- Green Sea
- Medium Flesh
- Rouge
- Santa's Flesh
- Village Green
- Wedgewood Green
- White
- Woodland Night Green

Loew-Cornell brushes
- Series 7050 10/0 script liner
- Series 7300 no. 12 flat shader
- Series 7500 no. 4 filbert
- Series 7550 ¾" wash brush

snake gourd
Delta Ceramcoat Sparkle Glaze
Delta Waterbased Sealer
glitter
Delta Color Float
two seashells
½"-thick birch plywood
Delta wood glue
Delta Ceramcoat Satin Interior
  Spray Varnish

GOURD PREPARATION

Slice off the bottom of the gourd on the bandsaw. Trace the tail pattern on the plywood, stand the gourd up on it at the end and trace around the end of the gourd to adjust the pattern to fit. Trace around the piece you cut off and, allowing for the thickness of the gourd, cut a circle of wood to fit inside the gourd. Once you have a snug fit, glue this piece inside. Allow to dry overnight. Glue the tail to the bottom of the gourd, pointing it in the direction of any overhang the gourd may have (see photograph). If you don't feel this is going to be enough weight to make the gourd stand, fill the gourd with approximately a pound of sand or birdshot before gluing the disk of wood inside the gourd.

BASECOAT

Seal gourd and let dry. Apply the pattern minus details. Basecoat hair Cloudberry Tan and White 1:1, flesh areas Medium Flesh, tail Wedgewood Green, seaweed Green Sea and water Woodland Night.

When dry, transfer the pattern details. Basecoat seahorses Dunes Beige and the mermaid's lips Rouge.

FACE AND HAIR

Shade hair with Antique Gold and highlight with Custard. The body and face are shaded with Desert Sun Orange and highlighted with Santa's Flesh. Float Desert Sun Orange down each side of her nose, over her eyelids (fading up), under the chin, in the armpits and inside the belly button. Float Santa's Flesh down the bridge of the nose, across the top of the eyes (fading up) and on the tip of the nose. Muriel's eyes are Village Green with a touch of Woodland Night, with Black pupils.

TAIL

Use Dark Forest Green to shade in the crevices of the tail and under the scales, Chrome Green Light for highlights and a mix of Wedgewood Green and White 1:1 for further highlighting.

FINISHING

Shade the seaweed along the edges and in the folds with Alpine Green and highlight with a mix of Green Sea and White 1:1. The seahorse is shaded with Dark Flesh and highlighted with Dunes Beige and White 1:1. Finish with several light coats of spray finish. Brush Sparkle Glaze over the tail and seashell bra. While still wet, sprinkle glitter on the bra.

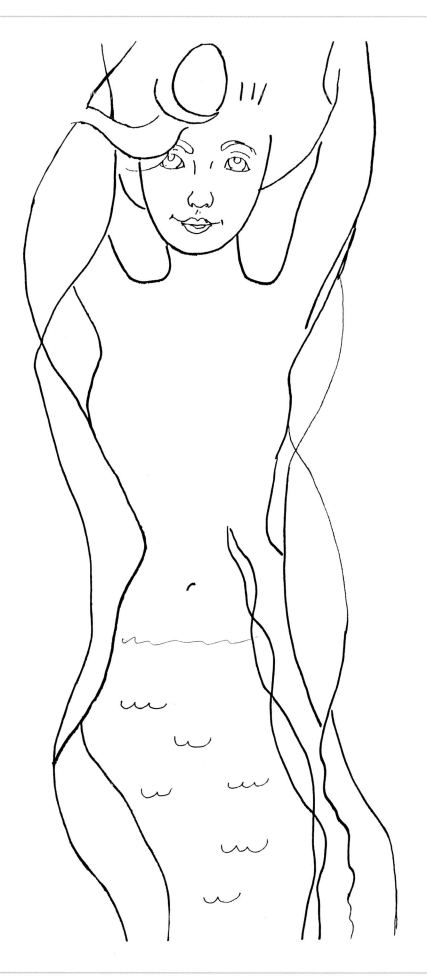

Gourd Fun for Everyone

Adjust to fit your gourd.

Mermaid back

Enlarge this pattern to fit your gourd. Every pattern may require adjustments to follow the contours of your particular gourd.

I was trying to look at things from a differ-ent point of view when I got the idea to turn a dipper gourd upside down instead of using it in the traditional manner.

materials

Delta Ceramcoat acrylics

- 14K Gold
- Bambi Brown
- Black
- Black Cherry
- Blue Spruce
- Bridgeport Grey
- Burnt Sienna
- Calypso Orange
- Cape Cod Blue
- Cinnamon
- Desert Sun Orange
- Leprechaun
- Light Ivory
- Medium Flesh
- Opaque Red
- Rainforest Green
- Rouge
- Santa's Flesh
- Silver Pine
- Tangerine
- White

Loew-Cornell brushes

- Series 7050 10/0 liner
- Series 7300 nos. 2, 4, 12 flat shaders
- Series 7520 ½" filbert rake
- Series 7850 ¼" deerfoot
- Series 7550 ¾" wash brush

dipper gourd
egg gourd
shield gourd
seven star buttons
FIMO boot mold
assorted miniature toys
Delta Color Float
FIMO clay, black
"thick 'n thin" yarn
glue gun
Delta Waterbased Sealer
gold string
wooden star
wooden dowel
½" thick plywood
Delta wood glue
Delta Acrylic Gloss Finish Spray

one-legged santa

PREPARATION

Cut star from ½" plywood. Drill a hole in center and glue in a wooden dowel approximately 6" long. Cut the stem end of the dipper gourd off, slip over the dowel and glue. Cut off end of egg gourd and glue on top of dipper gourd. Cut off end of shield gourd and glue on top of egg gourd. Mold and bake boots per package instructions. When cool, whittle the backs off to make them fit against the dipper base.

BASECOAT

Seal all pieces. Apply only basic parts of pattern and basecoat. The hat, coat, pants and edge of star are

Enlarge this pattern to fit your gourd. Every pattern may require adjustments to follow the contours of your particular gourd.

Opaque Red. Basecoat the top of star first in Bambi Brown, then 14K Gold. The cuffs, cap and jacket bands, candy canes, goose and front of jacket are White. Mitts are Black. The face is Medium Flesh and the hair and beard are Bridgeport Grey.

HAT, TUNIC AND PANTS

Float Black Cherry in a spiral around the hat, fading up. Float Tangerine back to back against the Black Cherry, fading down. Float Black Cherry around arms and down the front and back of the dipper stem to separate legs. The squares on the jacket and cap are sponged Opaque Red. The lines are Blue Spruce, and the dots are 14K Gold and Opaque Red. Stars on jacket are also 14K Gold.

DETAILS

Stripe candy canes with Opaque Red, then float Cape Cod Blue along the

edges. Paint a thin White line down the center of each cane. The goose's beak is Calypso Orange shaded with Tangerine. Its cap is Silver Pine shaded with Rainforest Green. The pompom is stippled on with the deerfoot using Blue Spruce, then Rainforest Green and Silver Pine. The snowflakes are Blue Spruce.

FACE AND HAIR

Apply face pattern and outline features with Burnt Sienna. Fill eyes in solid with White. Irises are Leprechaun, pupils Black. Shade face with Desert Sun Orange; highlight with Santa's Flesh. Fill nostrils and mouth with Cinnamon. Use the rake brush and White to make hair. Fill in eyebrows with the liner brush, using choppy strokes of White over Bridgeport Grey. Float Rouge across cheeks from ear to nose, fading up.

FINISHING

Finish with several light coats of spray finish. Use glue gun to attach star buttons back-to-back on gold string. Run strings through holes of one button and attach that button to end of cap. Glue boots to base of gourd and surround with assorted toys. Loop yarn back and forth and glue into place for beard and mustache.

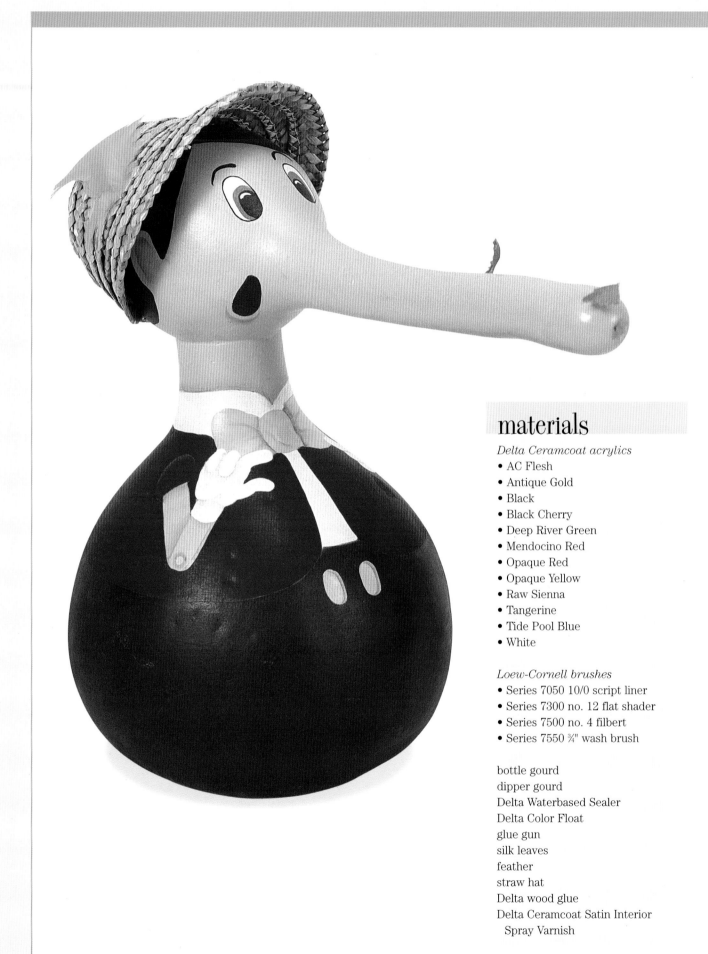

materials

Delta Ceramcoat acrylics
- AC Flesh
- Antique Gold
- Black
- Black Cherry
- Deep River Green
- Mendocino Red
- Opaque Red
- Opaque Yellow
- Raw Sienna
- Tangerine
- Tide Pool Blue
- White

Loew-Cornell brushes
- Series 7050 10/0 script liner
- Series 7300 no. 12 flat shader
- Series 7500 no. 4 filbert
- Series 7550 ¾" wash brush

bottle gourd
dipper gourd
Delta Waterbased Sealer
Delta Color Float
glue gun
silk leaves
feather
straw hat
Delta wood glue
Delta Ceramcoat Satin Interior
 Spray Varnish

pinocchio

Just look at that nose! This fellow is bound to delight any small ones you know—and teach them a lesson at the same time. Pinocchio is easy to make, because there is very little shading. The hardest part will be deciding how long to make the nose!

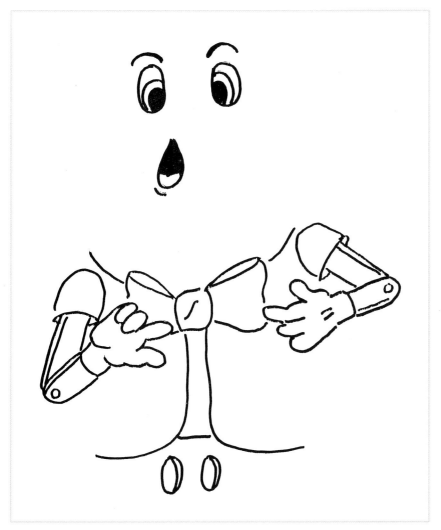

PREPARATION AND BASECOAT
Cut top off bottle gourd and glue dipper gourd on at right angle. Allow to dry overnight. Seal gourd and allow to dry. Apply pattern. Basecoat flesh areas with AC Flesh. Basecoat shirt and gloves White, pants Deep River Green, jacket Opaque Red, tie and buttons Opaque Yellow, hair and eyebrows Black, eyes White, tongue Mendocino Red, inside mouth Black, eyes Tide Pool Blue and pupils Black.

SHADING AND HIGHLIGHTING
Shade flesh areas with Raw Sienna. Jacket is shaded with Black Cherry and highlighted with Tangerine. Repaint tie and buttons Opaque Yellow and shade with Antique Gold.

FINISHING
Spray with several light coats of spray finish. Glue feather on hat, glue hat on head and glue leaves on nose.

Enlarge this pattern to fit your gourd. Every pattern may require adjustments to follow the contours of your particular gourd.

Here's a quick and clever project that's sure to please. Don't limit yourself to Santa! You can make several necklaces and add reindeer and elves. How about a Halloween theme with scarecrows and jack-o-lanterns? Let your imagination be your guide.

Gourd Fun for Everyone

santa necklace

materials

Delta Ceramcoat acrylics
- Black
- Bridgeport Grey
- Burnt Sienna
- Candy Bar Brown
- Cinnamon
- Desert Sun Orange
- Leprechaun
- Medium Flesh
- Normandy Rose
- Opaque Red
- Rouge
- Storm Grey
- White

Loew-Cornell brushes
- Series 7350 10/0 liner
- Series 7300 no. 12 flat shader
- Series 7520 ½" filbert rake

egg gourd
glue gun
narrow ribbon
jingle bells
strong thread
Delta Color Float
Delta Waterbased Sealer
Delta Ceramcoat Satin Interior
  Spray Varnish
three 2"-wide, 45" long strips of
  Christmas fabric in red, green
  and white

BASECOAT
Seal gourd and let dry. Apply pattern and basecoat hat Opaque Red. Basecoat face Normandy Rose and all hair areas Bridgeport Grey.

SANTA PENDANT
Transfer features and outline with Burnt Sienna. Fill nostrils and mouth with Cinnamon. Fill eyes in solid with White. The iris is Leprechaun and the pupil is Black. Place the White highlight in the eye with the liner. Shade wrinkles with Desert Sun Orange and highlight with Normandy Rose and White 1:1. Use the rake brush and White to make hair and beard. Fill in eyebrows with the liner using choppy strokes of White. Float Rouge across the face from ear to nose, fading up. Finish with several light coats of spray finish.

NECKLACE
Braid the three strips of material, leaving about 3" loose at each end. Tie off with the thread, then tie the two ends together. Make a bow with several loops of ribbon and tie bells to the ends. Glue the bow on over the thread where the two ends meet, then glue the egg gourd to the center of the bow.

A larger Santa makes a great ornament. Be sure to make enough.

Santa's Face

Here's a worksheet that will help you get your Santa faces just right.

Enlarge this pattern to fit your gourd. Every pattern may require adjustments to follow the contours of your particular gourd.

Santa's Eyes

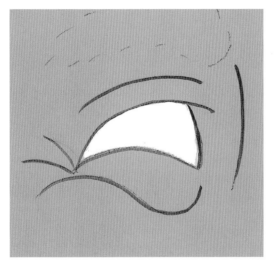

1 Basecoat face in Medium Flesh. Apply the pattern. Outline features using a 10/0 liner and thinned Burnt Sienna. Fill the eyes in solid with White. Now is the time to check the eyes. Are they level? The same size?

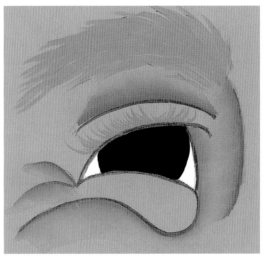

2 Fill the pupils in solid Black. Always use the largest brush that you can comfortably fit into the space. The larger the brush, the fewer the streaks. This is especially true when basecoating. *Hint:* If you are right handed, paint the left eye first. You'll find it much easier to match them.

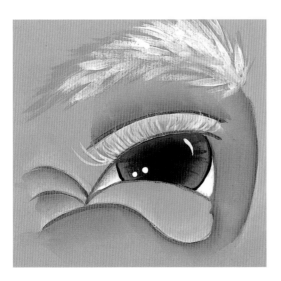

3 Using a no. 12 flat and your choice of eye color, float down each side of the pupil leaving a tiny black line at the edge. Pull a few darker lines of the same color. When dry, float a shadow of Storm Grey across the eye just below the eyelid fading down. Add a White highlight in the exact same place in each eye.

Santa's Face

1 Basecoat Santa's face as described in the first step of Santa's Eyes.

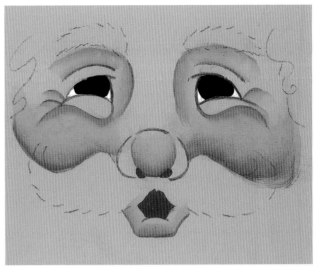

2 Using a no. 12 flat and Desert Sun Orange, shade the wrinkles, lip, down each side of the nose and under the eyebrow. Keep the hard edge up, fading down. Be sure to taper the ends of the shadows. Float Rouge across the cheeks from ear to nose and across the bottom of the nose. Tap lightly with a mop brush to soften.

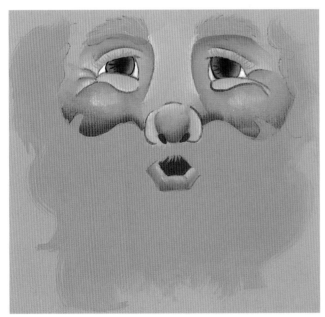

3 Use Santa's Flesh to highlight eyelids, bridge of nose, nostril covers, wrinkles and the top of the lip. Slightly moisten the cheeks, tap in a little highlight, then mop. Fill mouth and nostrils with a mix of Desert Sun Orange and Candy Bar Brown 1:2. Basecoat eyebrows, hair, beard and mustache in Bridgeport Grey. Keep the edges shaggy so you don't have a hard line to overcome later. The filbert rake brush works great for this.

4 Using a filbert rake and thinned White, paint over the gray areas. Resist the urge to keep adding White. Don't lose your gray "shadows." If it's too gray when you finish, glaze the entire area with White. Float a Bridgeport Grey shadow under the nose and under the mustache and mouth. Use a 10/0 liner and thinned White to pull defining hairs where needed.

Gourd Fun for Everyone

stone cottage

materials

Delta Ceramcoat acrylics
- Black
- Black Green
- Bridgeport Grey
- Candy Bar Brown
- Custard
- Dark Forest Green
- Fiesta Pink
- Georgia Clay
- Green Sea
- Hammered Iron
- Hippo Grey
- Leaf Green
- Lichen Grey
- Maple Sugar Tan
- Midnight Blue
- Nightfall Blue
- Putty
- Quaker Grey
- Raw Sienna
- Sandstone
- Straw
- Territorial Beige
- White

Loew-Cornell brushes
- Series 7050 10/0 liner
- Series 7300 no. 12 shader
- Series 7550 ¾" wash brush

martin house gourd about 8"
 diameter
Delta Color Float
Delta Waterbased Sealer
Delta Ceramcoat Satin Interior
 Spray Varnish

I never include people in my cottages. If you don't see anyone in the windows or in the yard, you can imagine anyone living there! Don't let all the detail in this project intimidate you. Just follow the instructions, and you will see how easy it really is.

Here's a variation on the stone cottage.

BASECOAT

Seal gourd and let dry. Apply only roof and ground lines of pattern. Basecoat roof Maple Sugar Tan, house Quaker Grey and ground Dark Forest Green. Apply balance of pattern. Float Hippo Grey in circles, fading toward the center, for the stones. Fill crevices with Charcoal. Stipple Lichen Grey, Dark Forest Green and a little White on stones.

SHADE AND HIGHLIGHT

Shade roof with Raw Sienna and highlight with Custard. Pull fine lines with both colors to indicate thatch. Basecoat door, shutters and window frames with Putty; shade with Territorial Beige. Basecoat inside windows with Nightfall Blue; shade around inside of windows with Midnight Blue. Door hinges and handle are Hammered Iron. Curtains are a float of White.

DETAILS

Sponge bushes around the cottage with Black Green. Sponge Green Sea over that, leaving a little of the Black Green showing. Flowers are White with Straw centers. Flowerpot is Georgia Clay shaded with Candy Bar Brown. Flip-float Putty down the center to highlight. Basecoat tree White and shade with Bridgeport Grey. Lines are Charcoal. Sponge on leaves in Black Green, then Green Sea. Highlight with a little Leaf Green.

Finish with several light coats of spray finish.

Enlarge this pattern to fit your gourd. Every pattern may require adjustments to follow the contours of your particular gourd.

Construct this shoe by gluing gourds together.

Mortared Stones

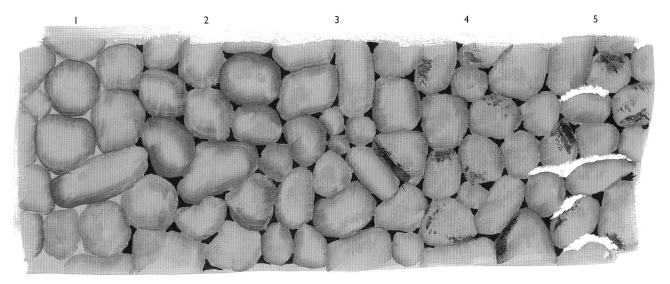

1 Basecoat with Quaker Grey. Using a no. 12 flat shader, float irregular circles of Hippo Grey. Keep the gaps between the stones to a minimum.

2 Using a 10/0 liner and thinned Charcoal, fill in between the stones. Take care not to create points on them. Notice that the mortar does not go all around the stones.

3 Using a deerfoot stippler or an old scruffy brush, dab Lichen Grey "dirt" randomly on some of the stones. Pat with a mop or your finger to soften.

4 Repeat step 3 using Dark Foliage to make moss.

5 If this is a winter scene, repeat step 3, placing White on the top edges of some stones.

You can even create a Christmas gourd!

Doors

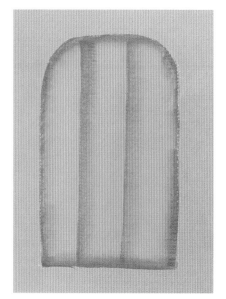

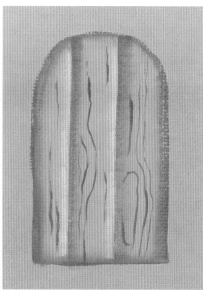

1 Basecoat door Trail. Shade around edge and between boards with Territorial Beige.

2 Highlight with Putty. Use a 10/0 liner and Territorial Beige to make wood grain.

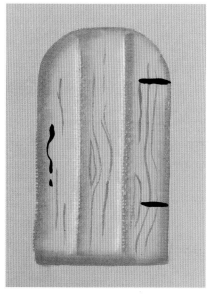

3 The handle and hinges are Black.

Birch Trees

TRUNK AND BRANCHES

1 Basecoat tree in White. Where the branches join the trunk, be sure you have U shapes, not V shapes.

2 Float a shadow of Bridgeport Grey down both sides of the trunk and on any branches that cross behind another branch.

3 Use a 10/0 liner brush and thinned Bridgeport Grey to make random horizontal marks on the bark. Curve them slightly to heighten the appearance of roundness. Add a few streaks of Hippo Grey.

FOLIAGE

4 Use a sea sponge to sponge Dark Foliage in the branches for leaves.

5 Next sponge Medium Foliage, leaving some of the previous color showing.

6 Next sponge Light Foliage sparingly and nearer the tops of the leaves for highlight.

Thatched Roof

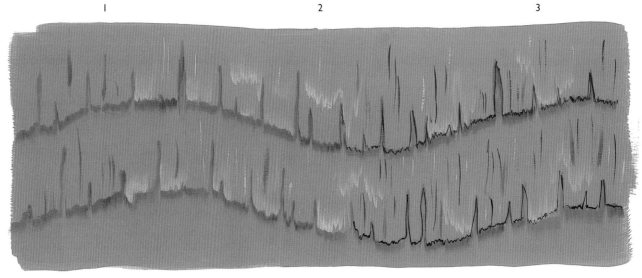

1 Basecoat the roof Palomino. With the hard edge up, float a ragged shadow of Raw Sienna under each row of thatch. Use the 10/0 liner to pull random lines.

2 With the hard edge down, highlight with Old Parchment.

3 Use the 10/0 liner and thinned Brown Iron Oxide to outline edges. Pull random lines.

Shingle Roof

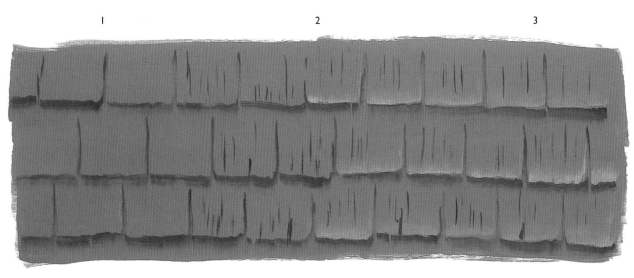

1 Basecoat the roof Cape Cod. With the hard edge up, float a shadow of Nightfall Blue under the bottom of the shingles and up one side.

2 Use the 10/0 liner to pull random lines of Nightfall Blue.

3 With the hard edge down, float a highlight of Lavender Lace along the bottom edge and up the opposite side of each shingle.

Curtains

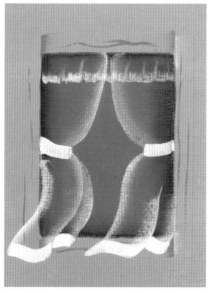
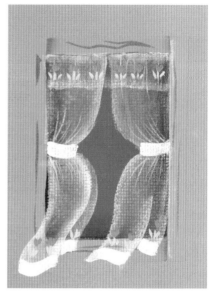

1 Basecoat the inside of the window Liberty Blue. Float a shadow of Midnight Blue around the edges.

2 Float the curtains in White using a no. 12 flat shader. Use a no. 2 flat to make the tiebacks and hems.

3 When dry, glaze the curtains with White, The flowers are Coral, the stems Village Green.

Flower Pot

1 Basecoat the flower pot in Georgia Clay.

2 Shade with Candy Bar Brown. Stipple in Dark Foliage, then Light Foliage.

3 Highlight with a flip float of Putty down the center of the pot. Glaze with Georgia Clay.

index

American Gourd Society, 3

Back-to-back float. *See* Double float
Basecoat, 8
Blow dryer, 16
Border, 19
Brush
    caring for, 15–16
    dirty, 8
    floating or side-loading, 9
    handle, 34, 59, 80, 91
    hints for using, 19
    large, 27, 118
    overloading, 19
    See also specific types of brushes
Brush blending, 8
Bullseye, 8

Chisel edge, 8
Clay, 89–91
Comma stroke, 40, 52, 71, 81
Crackle medium, 8
Cracks, repairing, 57
Craft lathe, 33
C-stroke, 77. *See also* Comma stroke

Dabbing, 8
Dalton Farms, 14
Deerfoot brush, 19, 49, 123
Dip dot, 8
Dolly Parton heart, 8, 59
Double float, 8
Double load, 8
Dowel
    gluing, 59, 113
    sharpening, 61, 63
Dress, 8
Drilling hole, 44, 58, 59, 63, 95
Drybrush, 8
Drying gourd, 17

Extender, 8–9, 12

Facial features, 26–27, 39–42, 51–52,
    58–59, 64, 70–71, 76–77, 85, 97, 109,
    117–119
Fading down, 51–52, 113, 118–119
Fading up, 26, 51–52, 102, 113
Ferrule, 9
Filbert rake brush, 59, 97, 119
Flat shader brush, 70, 78
Flip float, 102, 122. *See also* Double float
Float stroke, 9, 19

Flow medium, 9
Fly specking. *See* Spattering

Gesso, 9
Glaze, 9, 127
Glazing medium, 9–10
Glue, 81, 98, 113
Gold leaf, 10
Gouache, 10
Gourds (types of)
    apple, 13
    basketball, 13
    bat, 75, 97
    bottle, 13, 23, 37, 47, 61, 114
    bushel, 13
    cannonball, 13
    canteen, 13, 101
    Chinese bottle, 13, 47, 61
    club, 84
    coyote, 57
    dipper, 13, 105, 112, 114
    egg, 13, 33, 69, 89, 112, 117
    Indonesian bottle, 23
    long-handle dipper, 13
    martin house, 13, 121
    shield, 112
    snake, 13, 93, 109
    spoon, 13
    zucca, 13

Hard edge, 10

Lettering, 44, 53
Liner brush, 10, 19, 34
Loading. *See* Dress

Masking, 10
Materials, list of, 14. *See also* entries for
    specific materials
Mirror float. *See* Double float
Mixture ratio, 19
Mop, 10, 19, 65, 97

National Society of Decorative Painters, 3

Palette paper, 16
Paper towel, 16
Pattern, transferring, 18, 25
Pickling, 10
Plywood bottom, 18, 109
Pounce, 27. *See also* Dabbing; Stippling
Primer, 10
Pull, 10

Rake brush, 11, 19, 41
Retarder. *See* Extender, 10
Reverse float. *See* Double float
Ribbon, 95
Rubber stamp, 98

Sanding, 18, 63
Saw, 57
Scruffy brush, 10, 49, 123
Scumbling. *See* Stippling
Sealer, 10, 18
Sealing, 25
Shading, 27–28. *See also* Float stroke
Side-loading, 9, 10. *See also* Floating
Sitdowns, 10, 35
Slip-slap, 10
Soft edge, 10
Spattering, 10, 98
Sponge, 11, 27, 124
Stippling, 11, 49–50
Stitching details, 30, 43
Stripes, 33–34, 98, 105, 113
Stylus, 11, 26, 31, 35, 86

Tack cloth, 11
Tinting. See Glaze
Tools, list of, 14. *See also* entries for spe-
    cific tools
Tooth, 12
Transfer, 11
Transfer paper, 12
Triple load, 12

Undercoat, 12

Varnish, 12, 16

Walking color, 12
Washing gourd, 17
Water tub, 16
Wet on wet, 12
Wire, 90, 98